THE BIOSOCIAL BASIS

OF MENTAL RETARDATION

THE
BIOSOCIAL BASIS
OF MENTAL
RETARDATION

EDITED BY

SONIA F. OSLER AND ROBERT E. COOKE

THE JOHNS HOPKINS PRESS

BALTIMORE, MARYLAND

TO JOHN F. KENNEDY FOR HIS RECOGNITION
OF THE NEEDS OF THE MENTALLY RETARDED

PREFACE

The exposure of pre- and postdoctoral medical students to teaching in mental retardation has been extremely limited until recently. In 1960, a seminar course in mental retardation was established at the Johns Hopkins University School of Medicine as an attempt to bring to students of medicine recent scientific developments in a field of great national concern. This course was developed as part of the research and training program in mental retardation supported by the Joseph P. Kennedy, Jr., Foundation, which has provided construction funds, support of senior scholars in research in developmental neuro-anatomy, placental physiology, prenatal virology, neurochemistry, and enzymology, as well as research funds for the initiation and development of new experimental projects.

For the first two years the course covered general aspects of mental retardation, varying from epidemiologic studies to neuroanatomical problems. In 1963, the course was altered to present in depth certain facets of this extraordinarily broad field. Advances in the biochemical aspects of mental retardation were presented at that time. In 1964, the behavioral aspects of mental retardation were presented in a series of

Sonia F. Osler, Ph.D., is associate professor of pediatrics and medical psychology, The Johns Hopkins University School of Medicine. Robert E. Cooke, M.D., is professor and director of the Department of Pediatrics, The Johns Hopkins University School of Medicine, and pediatrician-in-chief, The Johns Hopkins Hospital.

vii

weekly seminars with extensive discussion thereafter. Particular emphasis was placed on the possible relationship between biological and social factors in producing mild degreees of retardation.

The excellent assembly of lecturers, the enthusiastic response of the very large audience, and the numerous requests for reproduction of this course have led to the publication of this book. The work has been edited primarily by Dr. Sonia F. Osler, whose familiarity and interest in cognitive studies in mental retardation made the task pleasurable and the results rewarding. It is hoped that this volume will stimulate behavioral scientists to view their own research in a way that might be applicable to the prevention, diagnosis, treatment, or education of the mentally retarded.

SONIA F. OSLER
ROBERT E. COOKE

Baltimore, 1965

CONTENTS

INTRODUCTION

Despite the growing knowledge about its multiple and complex etiology and the availability of more refined techniques for psychological assessment, mental retardation continues to be regarded, in the main, as a rather generalized and homogeneous state of inadequate intellectual functioning. Differentiations among the retarded continue to be made along a quantitative continuum, which yields a classification based primarily on the degree of deficit, ranging from borderline defectives who can generally function in the community to those individuals who are completely dependent upon custodial care.

It seems apparent that the global approach to mental retardation has failed to stimulate studies designed to delineate differences of a qualitative nature between individuals within a currently specified category of mental retardation. Mental retardation research has been largely confined to group comparisons of retarded and normal subjects on tasks involving learning, discrimination, problem solving, and perceptual processes. This type of research, it is generally admitted, has not produced valid generalizations as to the nature of intellectual defect. Data, carefully garnered, have resisted meaningful summarization and integration, even in areas that are amenable to standardized assay techniques, such as sensory function.

The difficulties encountered with the research data have been variously attributed to inadequate experimental controls, lack of uniformity in research methodology, poor definition of relevant variables, or paucity of data. While these factors have undoubtedly contributed to the general state of the field, we wish to point to another possible source of difficulty to account for the current situation, namely, the tacit assumption that mental retardation is qualitatively similar within all individuals at a given level of defect. The basis for the assumption of intellectual homogeneity can probably be ascribed to the use of the IQ score as the diagnostic criterion for mental deficiency. While the inadequacy of the IQ criterion has been discussed at length by many, little has been said about the implications of its use for research methodology in mental retardation.

An alternative assumption would posit variations in the kinds of fundamental intellectual defects to be found among the mentally retarded. The rationale for this assumption stems from the diversity of etiologic factors in mental retardation, the varieties of defects associated with brain lesions (including various forms of aphasia), and the findings resulting from experimentally induced states of deprivation. It seems more reasonable (as well as more parsimonious) to conjecture that causative factors as diverse as chromosomal trisomy and cultural deprivation might well exert different effects on central nervous system function than to assume identical effects which are independent of the implicated agent.

If mental retardation is to be viewed as a group of defects resulting in impairment of intellectual function, then the usual comparisons between random groups of retarded and normal individuals run the risk of obscuring differences in function because of inappropriate subject selection. If, for example, there may be found within a group of defectives those whose underlying difficulty stems from impairment of sensory processing, others with a basic language deficit, and still others with profound disturbances in memory, an experimental task which depends primarily upon sensory discrimination might suffer one fate with subjects whose memory is defective and quite another with those whose sensory input is inadequately processed, in much the same way as Harlow's socially deprived monkeys (Chapter 5) showed no learning deficit on discrimination problems, while Riesen's light-deprived monkeys (Chapter 4) were probably capable of adequate mothering behavior. Group comparisons of performance on any one type of task in which the subjects may suffer from diverse types of defective states are therefore likely to yield ambiguous results. The degree of ambiguity will depend on the kinds of functions which the experimental task involves and the degree of heterogeneity of subject groups.

The predication of a variety of defective intellectual states implies a change in research strategy. In place of group comparisons, intensive intra-individual studies might be undertaken as a possible basis for arriving at a typology of mental defect. The further advantage of intra-individual studies is that they may yield information on the distribution of specific defects in the retarded population as well as the tendency for groups of defects to occur in clusters. The study of clusters may in turn provide clues as to the hierarchical organization of intellectual functions.

The search for qualitative differences in impaired behavior need not be confined to intra-individual studies. Other approaches, such as the experimental induction of deprived states, are illustrated in the investigations described in the essays comprising this volume. The goal of the original lectures on which the essays are based was to assemble from a variety of disciplines objective data pertaining to the effects of biological and social deprivation on cognitive development. The term deprivation was interpreted broadly to include all serious deviations from optimal requirements for growth and development, ranging from disturbed biochemical states, such as anoxia, to social isolation from contact with peers. Cognition refers in general to the adaptive functions involved in perception, learning, problem solving, conceptualization, and symbolic behavior. The individual contributions, which include data from animal and human studies, come from a variety of disciplines: economics, education, pediatrics, as well as comparative, physiological, and experimental psychology. The research methodologies employed by the investigators range from social surveys, through prospective studies of development, to the experimental manipulation of variables for the observation of learning or the production of deprived states. Exhaustive coverage of the subject matter on the biological and social variables related to mental retardation was neither intended nor achieved.

The material can be readily separated into four sections. Introducing the first section, Ginzberg discusses the scope of the problem, the prevalence of mental retardation (or in his terms, educational inadequacy) in the United States, and deals with some of the associated sociologic and geographic variables. Proposals for ameliorating the problems of the intellectually handicapped and the responsibility they present for society are presented. Shaffer's historical review of the conceptions of intelligence integrates an unusually broad range of data bearing on such issues as the unitary nature of intelligence, the constancy of the IQ, and the genetic basis of intellectual capacity.

The second section describes the role of perinatal factors on subsequent cognitive function. Hardy discusses data collected in the Collaborative Perinatal Project relating the incidence of complications of pregnancy and delivery, as well as various types of biochemical imbalance in the neonate, upon intellectual function in the first four years of life.

An examination of experimentally produced sensory and social deprivations and their consequences comprises the third section of the book. A series of studies presented by Riesen on the effects of reduced stimulation on organic and behavioral growth in the visual system, together with Harlow's studies on the consequences of maternal and social deprivation, constitute a solid body of evidence for the critical role of stimulation in the development of the maturing organism.

The last portion of the book deals with the learning characteristics of the retarded and proposed remedial measures. Zeaman's data, which emphasize defective attention processes in the retarded, and Kirk's experiences with diagnostic and remedial measures may together provide a basis for designing educational programs addressed to the specific defects of mentally retarded individuals.

SONIA F. OSLER

THE BIOSOCIAL BASIS
OF MENTAL RETARDATION

1

THE MENTALLY HANDICAPPED
IN A TECHNOLOGICAL SOCIETY

Eli Ginzberg

I plan to do five things in this discussion. First, I will set out my understanding of certain parameters of the problem, and then present some selected data, old and new, which will describe the problem from a social scientist's point of view. Thirdly, I will speculate briefly about some of the underlying causes of mental handicaps. I also want to make explicit some of the characteristics of this technological society and its labor force demands. And finally, since I am a very immodest person, I will explain what I think ought to be done in research as an aid to policy-making.

First, with regard to the parameters, when anyone deals with such complex phenomena as the mentally handicapped, or the poverty stricken, or those who suffer from mental illness, or the delinquents, or any of these larger social constellations, it is very difficult, in fact almost impossible, to separate the genetic from the environmental components, short of the most delicate and elaborate type of research.

The second point, by way of introduction, is that in our country we deal with large figures. I suspect that we tend to blow up each of these categories to some extent in order to get public attention and, hopefully, some public action. We talk about the tens of millions of people who have chronic illness. What do these figures mean? We talk about fifteen to twenty million people who are emotionally unstable, and I don't know what that means. We talk about the many

ELI GINZBERG, Ph.D., is professor of economics and director of the Conservation of Human Resources Project, Columbia University.

1

millions who are alcoholics, and although I don't doubt that there are many millions who drink a lot, maybe too much, it's impossible to count them. Similarly, to talk about five million mentally retarded persons leaves me a little bit restive.

The third point is that although I have no pretense of competence in the area of mental testing, it does not appear logical to me to divide the continuum on the intelligence scale arbitrarily from seventy to fifty, then from fifty down to thirty. A continuum around points narrowly separated may have logic, but over that wide a range there are substantial orders of change. Now I don't know just where the end points come or how much of a jump one has to have for a change in diagnostic category, but in considering such a continuum, distinctions from the upper to the lower end should be made clearer.

The next point that is disturbing to an outsider is that of this large composite group of five million human beings who are supposed to fit one description, we understand the etiology of not more than 20 to 25 per cent of the total group. That is, we have defined a problem without any real diagnostic competence with respect to very large numbers within the categories. In the literature that I have seen there is a failure to distinguish the severely retarded human beings, who need constant supervision or very high orders of protection, from people in the community who have some difficulties in merely operating effectively in a competitive society. While at the points of contact between two such sub-groups there may be difficulties of differentiation and overlap, nevertheless, operationally, we can distinguish, and distinguish rather sharply, between the central distributions that belong to each of these two sub-categories.

Now I will discuss what we learned from two studies that we did ourselves, and a third study that the government has just published. Our analysis of the World War II data was first published in 1953 in *The Uneducated* (Ginzberg and Bray) and was based on the entire Selective Service experience of World War II broken down by counties. All the information about the educational and mental qualifications—and deficiencies—of all the people who were screened for military service in the United States in 3,000 counties was available to us. The same material was covered in a more refined fashion in the three-volume study called *The Ineffective Soldier* (Ginzberg *et al.*, 1959). The third reference is to a recently published government report called *One-Third of a Nation* (The President's Task Force on Manpower Conservation, 1964). This report consists of the analysis of a special sample of 3,000 Selective Service registrants.

The 1953 book contains an analysis of rejections for military service by regions divided into 9 classes, ranging from those with less than 25 rejected per 1,000 to those with over 200 rejected per 1,000 screened. Mapping these data reveals that the rate of rejection for intellectual deficiencies among the white registrants was strikingly high in the South and the Southeast, while the rate for Negroes outside of the South was not higher, and in some places was even lower, than the rates for whites.

For the United States as a whole, rejections for military service during World War II for mental or educational deficiencies were at the rate of 40 per 1,000. The average for whites was 25 per 1,000 and for Negroes it was 152 per 1,000. That was one type of gross difference. But the variability among the white population went from roughly 10 per 1,000 to 50 per 1,000. There was, then, a 500 per cent differential between the best states and the worst. The Negro differential was also fivefold, from 40 to 200 per 1,000. In Washington or Oregon, the rate of rejection was 5 per 1,000 for whites, compared with 55 per 1,000 in Kentucky, Tennessee, and North Carolina. This was an 11 to 1 variation among states. For the non-whites, New York State had a rejection rate of 36 per 1,000 for Negroes, and in South Carolina the rate was 277 per 1,000. This represents a variation in Negro rates among the states of 8 to 1. These few figures point up some of the findings based on the data of World War II.

What do we find in the new *One-Third of a Nation* report, which presents data for 1963? Let me introduce this by saying that the criterion used for rejection in World War II was an ability to read or write at fifth-grade level. Everyone who did not meet this criterion was classified as being illiterate. In the intervening years, and this brings us into a more advanced technological society, the armed services have been less pressed for manpower, their equipment has become more technical, and their tasks more complicated. In this period they have raised their literacy standards from fifth-grade to roughly ninth-grade. The present standards for induction into the armed services require about a ninth-grade educational level.

On the basis of this criterion, which is not the same as the earlier one, what do we find? Currently, one-third of all the youngsters reaching eighteen are rejected by the armed services for medical, mental, or administrative reasons. I repeat that the armed services are currently rejecting about a third of the relevant age population. Of those rejected for mental defects, about half are rejected because they fail the Armed Forces Qualification Test (AFQT). That is, one-half of one-third, or one-sixth, of all eighteen-year-olds in the United States are being rejected for military service because they do not meet the equivalent of a ninth-grade level of schooling.

Here again the variability among states is great. There is a twenty-to-one variability at the present time. In some of the states, South Carolina and Mississippi in particular, one out of every two young men eligible for military service is rejected because of mental handicaps. Those figures include both Negroes and whites. In Minnesota and the Northwest under 3 per cent are rejected. The Negro rates have not been published separately in this report, but I can say, from what I know of the data and my feel of them, that in Mississippi and South Carolina possibly as many as four out of five Negroes appearing for the examination cannot pass the ninth-grade test.

Although many of the facts we want to know remain obscure, there is one conclusion that is clear and unequivocal. A racial interpretation cannot be supported by these figures. While it is true that, on the whole, the white averages of rejection are far below the Negro averages, rates of rejection of Negroes in the northern states in World War II and, I would guess currently, are below the rates of rejection of the white population in some of the states in the South. Interestingly enough, that was true even in World War I.

In my study of the uneducated, the states were divided into quartiles on the basis of rejection rates by the armed services. For each quartile three factors were computed: educational expenditures, per capita income, and the degree of rurality. We found that there was a very close relationship between these factors and rejection rates. The states with the lowest expenditures for education had seven times more rejections than those with the highest expenditures. As for per capita income, the rich states had rejection rates only one-eighth those of the poor states, while the rates for the more urban counties were only one-seventh those of more rural counties. These three basic factors, educational expenditures, per capita income, and rurality, explained most of the variability among states. If we drop the Negro problem out of the picture completely and look simply at the white part of the story, the relation between the more favored and the less favored states is in the ratio of one to five in the respective rejection rates.

If we look at the most recent report, *One-Third of a Nation*, we first find that two out of five of the youngsters rejected on the basis of the AFQT never went beyond elementary school. Since the test requires achievement roughly the equivalent of the ninth grade, this is hardly surprising. The second finding is that four out of five did not finish high school. The third finding is that of those who were out of school, one out of three was unemployed at the time that he was examined. Since most of the selectees were twenty-one or twenty-two, an unemployment rate of 33 per cent is very high. Even though the unemployment rate for youth is very high these days—it runs at about 15 to 20 per cent—this was a differentially high rate.

Two more interesting findings show up. Seven out of ten rejectees came from families of more than four children. In the United States as a whole, only one-third of all the families have more than four children. But seven out of ten of these rejected youngsters came from very large families. One out of two came from families with six children or more. Only 10 per cent of all the families in the United States have six or more children, but they contributed 50 per cent of the rejectees. This unusual finding is even more significant when considered in conjunction with another piece of evidence: one out of two of the young men came from families with an income of less than $4,000. One out of five came from families with an income of less than $2,000.

It begins to appear that there is a heavy cycle of poverty: parents at the lower end of the social economic scale, producing youngsters who, in turn, do very poorly in school, drop out, and consequently perform poorly on this examination. The one difference between the present and the earlier data is the fact that 70 per cent of these youngsters were urban-reared. It would be useful to know whether these families were first generation migrants into urban centers. Social research has produced relatively little information on the differentiation of urban populations, including the problem populations of these centers. In general migrants have a difficult time; they come into the cities from the southern farms, or even the northern farms, and are handicapped in adjusting to modern city living. To what extent our urban problems arise from the problems of migrants and to what extent these problems are independent of migration has not been determined.

A similar question may be posed concerning the regional differences discussed earlier. It is well known that since the Civil War the North and South have experienced differential immigration of Europeans. Practically none of the European immigrants settled in the South. Nonetheless, the population in the South increased at a rate almost equal to that experienced by the North and the West through immigration. The growth of the southern population was achieved through a fantastic increase in the birth rate in the South after the Civil War. The major crop of the South is babies. The relationship, if any, between its expanding population and the other problems remains to be demonstrated.

I shall now discuss some questions concerning employment and the development of skills. The founder of economics, Adam Smith, begins his great book *The Wealth of Nations* with the statement that the skill and dexterity of the population is the key to the wealth of a nation. There is always a mutual accommodation between the economy and the qualities of the population. In 1945, I was in Peking, a city of a million and a half or two million. If an army car broke down in Peking at that time, the only people who could fix it were Japanese prisoners of war, because there had been no mechanical industrialized base to the Chinese culture of Peking. There are undoubtedly mechanics in Peking today; this is one adaptation which has taken place in the last fifteen or twenty years. The interplay between demands and skills helps to explain why in World War I the U.S. Army rejected only about 40,000 for mental deficiency while for a force only three times as large almost two million in World War II were put in special categories for educational defects. We are now rejecting one-sixth of the population for military service. The educational level of the population is constantly going up, but so are the skill needs of the economy and the military. They cannot go up indefinitely, of course. The armed services found in the Korean War, for instance, that signal equipment was not used because it was over-engineered and the soldiers found it was much easier to handle World War II equipment. Mistakes can be made, but basically the economy and the society as a whole adjust themselves to the average competences of the population. In passing, I have a suspicion that in medicine we have not made enough allowance for the fact that patients are more and more intelligent. A lot of physicians still think they are dealing with simple-minded immigrants who are basically illiterate, while actually many of their patients are relatively well-informed individuals.

We have a complicated society now with many technical gadgets, which produce difficulties for the handicapped. In an apartment house today there are stoves that use gas. This presupposes that everybody has enough competence to turn on the gas, or to turn it off, and not to get in trouble with these appliances. In a simple society, the opportunities for simple-minded people, or just simple people, to get themselves into trouble was more controlled because there were not so many potentially dangerous gadgets around. The fact that we murder 40,000 people a year on the highways is an indication of an imbalance between technology and the emotional maturity, if not the intellectual maturity, of the population. A very large number of the people who are killed annually on the highways are killed because of the fact that we have more powerful instruments in the hands of the population than the population is competent to deal with.

Historically the farm could absorb people with a great range of competence because it provided opportunities for a variety of tasks differing in amounts of skill and energy expenditures required. For example, a person who is sufficiently unbalanced emotionally, or not quite co-ordinated enough to remember always to button his trousers, creates no problem on a farm. But such a man cannot live in a city. The police would pick him up. An urban civilization makes demands for conformity and certain minimum standards. The farm is a wonderful place to absorb people of lesser competences and to fit them into the economy.

In our study of *The Ineffective Soldier* we have a series of life histories that gives some indication of how protective a farm environment was for many of these people. They went to a movie once a year with their parents and they did all right. That is not possible in the city. But because many of our farm youth have moved into Chicago and into New York and similar areas, a tremendous problem in adjustment and control has resulted.

The reason for the migration into the cities has to do with automation, which in my language simply means continuing technological change. What has happened is that successive technological changes have eliminated many of the simple jobs on the farm, reducing drastically the amount of unskilled labor required on the farm. The equipment is expensive and simple-minded persons cannot operate it. Automation then moved into manufacturing and eliminated not only the unskilled jobs but also some skilled jobs. We are now beginning to use machines in white collar and office work. A very large number of jobs of routine, repetitive nature will be eliminated in this area next. We cannot, fortunately, use machines in all of the service areas; but on the other hand, it is difficult to supervise people in the services, and this explains why so much service is of such poor quality. The nature of an affluent society, its income levels, the capital equipment that it works with, all make it increasingly difficult to absorb labor of modest skills. The fact that we tend to work in very large organizations, which make not only intellectual demands but all sorts of social demands, requires that we learn how to adjust to a large number of different supervisors, colleagues, and fellow workers. A lot of the people who broke down in the armed services just broke down, not because they were unintelligent, but because of the nature of this complex society. The military organization itself, just as any large organization, makes severe demands on people.

Another factor that will have adverse effects on individuals of low mental equipment is the job situation. Despite the prosperity, and it is a sizable prosperity in economic terms, the employment situation leaves much to be desired and will get worse for a very simple reason. In the past about 2.8 million youngsters turned eighteen per year. This year there will be 3.8 million, a jump of 1 million in a single year. If the young people do not get jobs this year, they will be looking for jobs next year. Each year the inflow will be at the new high level and, consequently, I take an ominous view of the problems of employment in the near future in the United States. I say this also with a certain amount of governmental authority as well as professional authority. I serve as the chairman of the National Manpower Advisory Committee and we are involved in a national retraining program. Of course, not everybody in the government shares my caution.

Given that kind of labor market the employer is obviously in a somewhat preferred position to pick and choose. Of course, this has been going on for a long time; the employer picks and chooses because of his heavy capital costs and the delicately articulated organization that he is trying to protect. The skill requirements in the current employment picture indicate that the total demand for people who have difficulty in learning and some difficulty in performing is quite limited.

Now for my few ideas about policy, both from the point of view of research and the point of view of action. The United States is now committed to a new dimension of social policy, which goes under the loose heading of a "war on poverty." We are going to try self-consciously to do something in the United States to mitigate conditions of those at the lower end of the distribution curve on income or any other basis. It doesn't matter at this point whether there are twenty million, or twenty-five million, or thirty million, or thirty-five million involved. There are too many people at that end and we are going to try to do something about it.

I hope that, if we are going to learn how to do something about the poverty stricken group, we will learn a lot about the antecedent

factors involved in poverty and what consequences poverty brings
with it. I hope that somewhere along the line we will begin to do
some epidemiological studies that will begin to throw new light on
the problem of the mentally handicapped in that connection. We are
going into communities like Appalachia, and this would be not a
bad time to learn something about the distribution of capacities of
youngsters of different ages in a very adverse environment of that
nature.

It is quite clear also that the United States is at an early stage, not
a late stage, of final resolution of its racial problem. The Negroes
represent a very deprived part of the community. But let me quickly
add that while many Negroes are poor, not all the poor are Negroes,
and not all Negroes are poor. For example, one-third of all the
Negroes in Chicago and on the West Coast have more income per
family than half of all the white families in Chicago or on the West
Coast. The notion that Negroes are a homogeneous group of twenty
million poverty stricken, uneducated people is wrong. Thus, here
is another area where we have a chance, for the first time, to learn
something about a particularly deprived sub-group in the population.

I would like to isolate the effects of genetic components, family
relationships, and community characteristics upon the ultimate functioning of the individual. It is not easy to differentiate among the
community and the family and the individual's own inheritance, but
we should try to see what we can learn about some of these factors.
One of the most serious problems I see about the mentally handicapped is that so often they have multiple handicaps. I learned this
in World War II. An individual with one handicap could make a
pretty good adjustment in the Army. But it was difficult to find a
place in the system for people with multiple handicaps. That raised
a very important research clue: it may well be that many of the
people who show up later in life as mentally handicapped (educationally deprived) are actually reflecting an antecedent handicap that
was not picked up. This includes youngsters who cannot hear or
see properly in the classroom as well as those who are too disturbed
to adjust to a teacher. These antecedent factors make learning impossible. Ordering of multiple handicaps and trying to understand
their relationship to the less severely handicapped mental group con-
stitutes a very important story. This leads to the importance of early
diagnosis and, let us say, to establishing priorities for intervention.

I hope that as part of our increasing affluence we are entering a
period in which the country will commit itself to devoting more of its

total wealth to doing more for the people who need help. It is a little indecent now that we are a country of two-car families to say that we want to be a country of three-car families. At some stage of the game the acquisition of additional appurtenances of wealth leaves something to be desired. I am hopeful, if only because we may choke ourselves to death with these machines, that there will be some opportunity now to reconsider the nature of services and the priority of services that are required. It seems to me that in a civilized society we ought to be concerned with those people who start life with severe handicaps and need special types of help.

My own view is that the outlook for employment of the mentally handicapped is not very good. I have read much of the literature on vocational rehabilitation of the mentally retarded and it is not very impressive. However, I will end on a happier note. If we have a tremendous stagnant pool and start a new vocational rehabilitation program, we skim the top and always get a pretty good return. In a big complicated economy with seventy-five million jobs, we can feed in a few handicapped people and show wonderful results. The problem is the degree of effort and energy and co-operation that is needed to "get a few people fed in." To competitively integrate the severely handicapped would appear to indicate too slight a pay-off.

The best way to get social action in a democracy is to work with the largest group possible. We have a society with a very large number of people with different handicaps. There are a large number of people who are emotionally unbalanced to a point where they cannot be integrated into a going organization. They may have an IQ of 160 but they do not fit in easily. There are large numbers of people with severe physical handicaps. We have very large numbers of older people, and will have more of them, who have less physical strength and poorer educational qualifications than the younger group coming into the labor market. The total constituency of handicapped people is very sizable.

I would like to forget what the nature of the handicap is for the moment and simply argue the proposition I tried to argue for years in many different ways: these people are entitled to a chance to make a contribution to the society of which they are a part, and the society has an obligation to try to create for them reasonable opportunities to perform. It is not feasible to do this in terms of a competitive market place. But it is perfectly feasible to do it in terms of a non-competitive market place. This is a major challenge to government. We need a political commitment to this end and we need the intellectual imagination to structure a market that will be a protected market, where very large numbers of people with handicaps can work at 70 per cent capacity, 60 per cent capacity, even 40 per cent capacity, in jobs that they can do and that society wants done and where the costs of organization are reasonable. There comes a point where the costs may be too great, but we are far from that.

It would not be easy to organize such a protected environment within a large metropolitan center, but this is a large country. Human beings need more human beings than their immediate family at some stage of development. One way to begin to resolve some of these problems is to be more imaginative about how these handicapped people can support each other. We have always done this in mental hospitals to some extent, and even in other hospitals. I don't know how many educationally deprived employees there are at Johns Hopkins, but there are many at Harkness and at Mount Sinai in New York. These hospitals provide protective environments.

We have to develop more institutions where it is possible to use people under less than fully competitive circumstances. First we must conceive of these problems as not exclusively medical or biological or genetic, and surely not primarily or solely economic or social. This is a problem to which all of the disciplines can contribute both conceptually and socially. Economics is in a particularly good position since, in a very real sense, it is concerned with work—we are concerned with inputs of effort and with social benefits. While we are looking for knowledge, nothing can go further to contributing to the amelioration of the problems of the mentally handicapped than more imaginative economic planning, so that these human beings can have a chance to work and function in the society at the levels of their competence.

QUESTIONS

Question: How many new difficulties will result from the high birth rates which we are now experiencing?

Ginzberg: I will try to give you not just one opinion, but two opinions. The dominant group of economists in the country is still fairly optimistic that the adjustments of the market place will take care of the employment problem. They argue that people do not have all the things they want, and as they get more money they will spend what they have and that will create more jobs and the job market will be adjusted. One of my conservative friends, my very brilliant colleague, Arthur Burns, makes a distinction between his general optimism and his fear that unemployment with respect to young people is a real problem. That is, he recognizes that there may be a problem of absorbing all the youngsters.

But the dominant school of economists told President Kennedy and President Johnson that all we had to do was to reduce the tax rates and everything would work out well. I belong to the opposite school. I think that the question of the absorption of the numbers of youngsters coming of working age, plus all the married women who want to work, plus the old people who don't want to stop working because they don't have enough money to live decently, represents a challenge to this economy. I will give you just two figures. We created an average of eight hundred thousand jobs per year in the last decade, and in order to keep the rate of unemployment where it is we have to increase new jobs by about 50 per cent. We need about one million three hundred thousand new jobs per year. I see no prospect whatever of increasing the number of new jobs by that order of magnitude.

I think we will work the other way: we will work to squeeze people out of the labor force, to reduce the number of new entrants into the labor force. We have already reduced the optional retirement age under social security to sixty-two. The President has a large number of plans about opening up youth camps and so on. I think we will make some adjustments on the supply side. But to create really adequate work opportunities will take considerably more planning than we usually do in this country.

Question: Can the private economy create all the jobs required or must the government do more?

Ginzberg: In *The Pluralistic Economy* (Ginzberg, Hiestand, and Reubens, 1965), basic figures are developed for the first time to prove that eight out of nine new jobs created in the 1950's were outside the private enterprise sector. Eight out of nine new jobs from 1950 to 1960 were either on government account or in nonprofit sectors, which includes an institution such as Johns Hopkins. A lot of adjustments will have to be made that go way beyond the simple adjustment of increasing incomes to create more jobs. There is a much more difficult set of relationships among the private economy, the nonprofit economy, and the governmental economy. I asked my taxi driver what was new in Baltimore. I said I had not been here for some years.

"Oh," he said, "a tremendous amount of building, a lot of urban renewal, a great deal of hospital construction." Here we have examples of private, government, and non-profit activities. I think we are in for some further adjustments.

On the point of shorter hours, I testified as early as last summer before a congressional committee, being in a distinct minority, in favor of shorter hours, not because I really thought that we could get shorter hours in order to create a lot of jobs immediately, but because I think that to move down on the hours of work is one of a whole series of adjustments we need. I would like to see us take some hours off the work week now. One of the reasons is that with shorter working hours we will have more leisure and recreational industries will develop. I don't expect that shorter hours themselves will create any large number of jobs in the short run. In the longer run it is a necessary adjustment and I'm in favor of starting now.

Question: Can we not use a lot of new people in the services except that we cannot allocate them? How do we balance supply and demand?

Ginzberg: In the United States, roughly thirty-five billion dollars a year is spent on the medical services industry. You ask whether we ought not spend very much more. It might be all right to spend forty-five billion, but many good people would say that would not be enough. My distinguished colleague at Harvard, Seymour Harris, has a new book out. He says that we are not spending enough money on medicine and health. But I am by no means sure of that. Just to put in more billions of dollars without asking what you are getting for each additional billion might not be meaningful. I am not very impressed with what we are getting per additional billion that we spend. I do not believe that we can cope with the problems of this industry just by pouring in more billions of dollars.

Now with regard to medical personnel. It is not true that too few people are interested in going into the medical service industries. For many years the deans of the medical schools said that they were not getting enough candidates for medical school. But they did not understand that they were dealing with a thin age group. Now of course, the thing has turned around and each successive year they will have more people to pick from.

It is even untrue that not enough girls go into nursing. A large number of young women do go into nursing. The trouble is they don't like to stay in nursing because nursing is not really competitive with either marriage or with easier types of jobs in the society. It is not really true to say that the supply of nurses is stringent, even narrowly defined in terms of new entrants. As a matter of fact, the ratio of nurses to the population has even increased. That means that the retention of nurses in the profession has been somewhat better. The heart of this problem relates to the organization of the medical services. The medical service industry is like a university. Nobody runs it. Everybody runs his section of it. Everybody tries to maximize his position in the larger scheme of things. If the dean of my school tried to get me to change my hours and it would inconvenience me slightly, he would have a major eruption on his hands. It cannot be rationalized. Nobody can tell anybody else to do anything in a hospital. And nobody can tell anybody else to do anything in terms of medical services in the city of Baltimore. So we have the Catholics going off and building hospitals, the Jews going off and building them, and the university wanting to snare bodies for study purposes, and so it goes.

What is needed is one of two types of approaches. We can decide to continue to operate in a substantially laissez faire economy and take the inefficiencies that are embedded in this kind of operation on the assumption that to control it would be worse. That is not an unreasonable conclusion. The alternative is to have medical and hospital authorities exercise some kind of control over the medical service structure. We might control new beds and move into other selective sectors. It is perfectly clear that the A.M.A. is not going to help us out. We need an intellectual leadership in this field. The professors of medicine should give us the intellectual leadership.

The basic dilemma is how to control or rationalize an industry in which the professional leadership, for whatever complicated reasons, doesn't move to control itself adequately. Otherwise, we will come to an illogical impasse—how do laymen control physicians?

Question: What do you think of the British system of quotas for the handicapped?

Ginzberg: I know a fair amount about the British system. Last year I participated on a panel at the annual meeting of the President's Committee on Employment of the Handicapped (1963). Then I took an anti-British position, but my second ideas are sometimes better than my first. The dilemma is this: by the time we find jobs for all the people with handicaps, older people, people who are educationally handicapped, and then the physically handicapped, there will be very few jobs that will be left untagged. I think this possible selection warrants more study than we have given it, but I would like to believe that the answer lies elsewhere. It lies in the forced expansion of sensible and useful work under a system of imaginative organization. It doesn't even have to be done by the government. I think a lot of this would be done better by nonprofit institutions and perhaps even by private enterprise institutions. I would be perfectly willing to consider methods under government contract. We buy missiles under all kinds of government contracts. Why shouldn't we buy the management of thousands or even millions of people in special employment situations? It's not easy to arrange this, but if we simply sit back and say it's not easy to do, more and more people are going to be neglected.

REFERENCES

GINZBERG, E., ANDERSON, J. K., GINSBURG, S. W., & HERMA, J. L. *The ineffec-tive soldier: lessons for management and the nation.* New York: Columbia University Press, 1959. 3 vols.

GINZBERG, E., & BRAY, D. W. *The uneducated.* New York: Columbia University Press, 1953.

GINZBERG, E., HIESTAND, D. L., & REUBENS, BEATRICE G. *The pluralistic economy.* New York: McGraw-Hill, 1965.

The President's Committee on Employment of the Handicapped. *Report of 1963 Annual Meeting.* [Washington: U.S. Government Printing Office, 1964.]

The President's Task Force on Manpower Conservation. *One-third of a nation.* [Washington: U.S. Government Printing Office, 1964.]

2

THE NATURE OF INTELLIGENCE

G. Wilson Shaffer

Questions of Definition. The nature of intelligence has received much attention from psychologists, but unfortunately a large number of contradictory conceptions of the term have been presented. Differences of belief are found also concerning the methods of measurement, the extent of modifiability through experience, and the implication of the data for human development. Satisfactory answers to the important questions about intelligence await a better understanding of the nature of intelligence. For example, we cannot satisfactorily talk about deficiencies of intelligence without some understanding of its nature. An early commission investigating the matter stated that an intelligent person was one who could manage himself and his affairs with normal prudence. Such a definition fails to consider the fact that the managing of affairs is not the same for all individuals. One individual may face particularly complicated experiences that require unusual ability while another has his affairs so well arranged for him that it becomes a relatively simple matter to manage them adequately. To judge the intelligence of these two individuals on the basis of success or failure in managing their affairs is to ignore the fact that there is an extremely wide variation in the responsibilities of individuals. Aside from that, the determination of the degree of success (or failure) which characterizes an individual's life is so formidable as to render useless a criterion in terms of success.

G. WILSON SHAFFER, Ph.D., is professor of psychology and dean, The Johns Hopkins University.

The term intelligence was not invented by psychologists, but has been used for centuries to indicate certain gross abilities. The variations of meaning attributed to the term may be gleaned by reviewing briefly its usage by some of the earlier investigators who are responsible for the development of tests of intelligence.

According to Ebbinghaus (1897), intelligence was the ability to combine the elements of experience, or the integrative ability. Binet (1908) considered judgment to be the most important factor of intelligence. His conception was broader than that of Ebbinghaus, including such factors as memory, reason, ability to compare, comprehension, use of number concepts, power to combine objects into meaningful wholes, and knowledge of common events. His search for a quantitative measure led to the development of the measurement of mental age. Spearman (Hart and Spearman, 1912–13) believed intelligence to be the ability to discriminate fine differences; Thorndike (1914) defined it as the sum total of special abilities. Stern (1914) believed adaptability to be of primary importance and defined intelligence as "a general capacity of an individual consciously to adjust his thinking to new acquirements—it is a general mental adaptability to new problems and conditions of life." He considered Binet's designation of intelligence in terms of mental age to be inadequate and argued that defect and superiority should be expressed in terms of a ratio of mental age divided by chronological age. This quotient he termed the intelligence quotient. Freeman (1926) has defined intelligence as the "faculty with which the subject-matter of experience can be organized into new patterns." In 1921, thirteen psychologists who had been active in developing testing methods assembled their views regarding the nature of intelligence, and such a wide variety of conceptions was presented that psychologists in general were inclined to use the term as a generic or trade name for the tests, and some went so far as to say that intelligence is whatever intelligence tests measure.

In the early examination of the nature of the intellect, the elementary units of the mental organization were thought of as *sensations* which by combination and association were organized into perceptions. These perceptions could be further elaborated and generalized into concepts. The function of the intellect was considered to be the building of perceptions out of sensations and the construction of conceptions from perceptions.

To accomplish its abstract function, the mind had at its disposal a number of "faculties," such as memory, judgment, attention, reasoning, and imagination. These faculties were thought to be like muscles, which could be developed by exercise. For example, if a man exercised his faculty of judgment on one problem, the effect of this practice would be to improve his judgment for any other kind of problem. This elaboration of the idea of mental faculties was called the *doctrine of formal discipline.*

In recent years Wechsler, who views intelligence as a composite of separate factors, has stated his position in the following manner:

Intelligence is the aggregate or global capacity of the individual to act purposefully, to think rationally, and to deal effectively with his environment. It is global because it characterizes the individual's behavior as a whole, it is an aggregate because it is composed of elements or abilities which, though not entirely independent, are qualitatively differentiable. By measurement of these abilities, we ultimately evaluate intelligence. But intelligence is not identical with the mere sum of these abilities, however inclusive. There are three important reasons for this: 1. The ultimate products of intelligent behavior are not only a function of the number of abilities or their quality, but also of the way in which they are combined, that is, upon their configuration. 2. Factors other than intellectual ability, for example, those of drive and incentive, enter into intelligent behavior. 3. Finally, while different orders of intelligent behavior may require varying degrees of intellectual ability, an excess of any given ability may add relatively little to the effectiveness of the behavior as a whole. It would seem that so far as general intelligence is concerned, intellectual ability as such merely enters as a necessary minimum.

(Wechsler, 1944)

Wechsler has elaborated the point that although intelligence is not the mere sum of intellectual abilities, the only way to evaluate it quantitatively is by the measurement of the various aspects of these abilities. He has discussed intelligence as a kind of energy that becomes evident in terms of the tasks it enables us to perform, such as making appropriate associations between events, drawing correct inferences from propositions, understanding the meaning of words, or solving mathematical problems.

With such differences in definition, it is natural that the bases of measurement should also vary. Consequently intelligence tests differ from one another in terms of the importance given to the verbal factor, psychomotor reactions, social comprehension, and so on. Facility in the use of symbols, in manipulating objects, or in dealing with human beings may be referred to respectively as abstract, practical, and social intelligence. Clearly, then, the score attained by an individual may depend to some degree on the type of the test used. It should be noted, however, that individuals scoring high on one type of test tend to obtain high scores on other tests. Thus, there appears the dual characteristic of human abilities—their specificity on one hand and their interdependence on the other.

The notion of the dual nature of intelligence was first presented by Spearman in 1904 (1932). From the observed correlations between various measures of intellectual performance he concluded that all intellectual activity contained some element or factor in common. This general factor or G, which Spearman considered as mental energy, played an important role in every mental act, although some acts were thought to depend upon it more than others. The differences in intelligence between people were determined by how much G they possessed. The variation in intelligence that was not explainable in terms of this general factor was attributed to specific factors, or S. There were many different specific factors. Not only did individuals differ in the strength of the G factor, and therefore in the amount of intelligence, but they also had different kinds and amounts of S factors. Two people of the same general intellectual level might have very different talents and deficiencies. But the important point for Spearman was how much of this general factor they had.

One of the sharpest critics of Spearman's two factor theory was Thorndike (1927), who believed that the intercorrelations studied by Spearman were often too small to test the question of a common factor. Instead of one kind of general factor, Thorndike maintained that there were a large number of separate factors contributing to intelligence. He argued that people differed not only in their ability to perform any specific act but also in the range of tasks within their capacity. Intelligence for him was more like a series of skills or talents. The intercorrelations between the various tests were seen as resulting from the features they had in common with each other, even though they were measures of different abilities. Despite this atomistic approach, Thorndike actually saw fit to classify intellectual activity into three broad types—social, concrete, and abstract.

In 1927, Thurstone (1929) initiated the study of the intellect through an analysis of intercorrelations between the various tests of intelligence along the lines of Spearman's earlier work. As a result of a statistical technique of factor analysis his conclusions differed from those of Spearman. Thurstone argued that intellectual performance was an expression of a number of primary factors rather than a common general factor. For him the goal of intelligence test construction was the isolation of the primary factors and the construction of tests that measured individually each of these factors.

For convenience in thinking it is possible to place the three theoretical approaches to the nature of the mental organization on a continuum. At one extreme lies the atomistic view of Thorndike's which stresses a large number of mental elements. These separate elements act in combination in any mental act and may seem to be general in nature because of common elements among the various intellectual tasks that people are required to do. At the other extreme is the global concept of Spearman, which suggests that some general quality of mental organization pervades every mental act, even though there may be specific abilities determining the unique quality of a particular individual's performance. And finally, between these two falls Thurstone's view that not one general factor, nor a large number of specific factors, but a small number of independent factors make up the mental process.

One of the chief limitations in the approaches discussed here concerns the fact that the correlation matrix from which all three theories are derived depends upon what tests are included. Intelligence can be inferred from certain kinds of activities which can be measured only through appropriate samples of behavior. The inclusion of tasks for the purpose of measuring these behaviors depends upon many complex considerations, not the least of which is one's cultural frame of reference. The entire argument tends to become circular, since the types of tests we include depend on our prior notion of what intelligence is. For example, if the correlation matrix contains no tests that depend on speed, then speed will not appear as a factor in our factor analysis. However, if we have decided in advance that speed is one of the variables our tests should measure, then it may appear as an important source of variation in the battery of tests.

Our popular system of providing a single estimate of intellectual capacity is consistent with Spearman's theoretical approach. The best test, says Spearman, is one that calls for the largest amount of the general factor, and the best test materials should therefore be those that have high intercorrelations. Each part of the test should be so thoroughly saturated with the general factor that the effects of the specific factors would be cancelled out. The most widely used tests today, the Wechsler Adult Intelligence Scale, the Wechsler Intelligence Scale for Children, and the Stanford-Binet, whose sub-tests are highly intercorrelated, follow that precept.

However, many psychologists are recommending that a single estimate of intelligence be abandoned. This view is consistent with Thurstone's assumptions concerning the nature of intelligence. For Thurstone, any single measure of intellectual capacity is inappropriate. What we should be obtaining is a profile showing the individual's scores in the several primary factors that have been established by factorial techniques. Psychologists with this point of view argue that we are not justified in adding scores that measure different functions, and that consequently a total score representing intelligence is not meaningful.

In the early days of modern psychology the opinion was held that mental acts should be divided into three types: cognitive, conative, and affective. The cognitive aspect referred to the process of knowing and included only the intellectual functions. The conative side of mental acts included all aspects of motivation. The term affective was used to designate the emotional side of behavior. Psychology developed the tendency to study these components of behavior independently of each other, or at least it tended to think of them separately. While some psychologists today are arguing that this is no longer a justifiable way to approach psychological problems, present-day thinking is still greatly influenced by this division. Although no one would ever have argued that problem-solving behavior did not require motivation, it is interesting that all our measuring instruments attempt to isolate intelligence from its motivational component. In effect, we have been trying to study intelligence with motivation and emotions controlled. The principal objection to this way of proceeding in the study of human intelligence is that it may actually lead us to overlook the nature of the total mental act. We are gradually moving away from the extreme position that there are such things as cognitive functions that are separate and distinct from affective and motivational ones. Those psychologists who are still willing to separate cognitive from affective and conative are beginning to speak of interactions between them. Others go even further and suggest that the distinction should be dropped altogether.

These considerations have led a number of psychologists to talk about what have been called "nonintellective factors" in intelligence. Wechsler pointed out that the factors extracted from the correlation matrices account for only about 60 per cent of the total variability in the test performance. This fact, he concludes, demonstrates the existence of factors that seem to be nonintellectual in nature. Interpreting evidence from a number of kinds of sources, Wechsler concludes that

". . . general intelligence is the function of the personality as a whole and is determined by emotion and conative factors . . . " (Wechsler, 1950).

According to Alexander (1935), these latter factors cover such items as interest in doing the task and persistence and desire to succeed, which he provisionally called "X" and "Z" factors respectively. The position might be taken, therefore, that intelligence tests do not measure all of intelligence, but that they do measure sufficient portions of it to enable us to have a fairly reliable index of the individual's capacity. The intelligence tests measure more than mere learning ability or reasoning ability. They measure, in addition, capacities which cannot be defined as either intellective or cognitive, but may be represented by factors such as "X" and "Z." Attempts to exclude these factors from a test have, in general, resulted in reducing its effectiveness as a measure of general intelligence.

Nature vs. Nurture. The nature vs. nurture controversy has persisted throughout the period of development of intelligence measures. Most of the theorists believed that intelligence was an inherited capacity, which could be considered as a basic dimension of the individual. This belief gave rise to the idea of a fixed intelligence throughout the life of the individual.

It was Francis Galton who led the movement to establish the heritability of intelligence. In his study *Hereditary Genius* (Galton, 1869) he presented evidence to show that in Great Britain men of great reputation and distinction came from a relatively small group of families. The study was, of course, open to the obvious criticism that being born in these families provided for them an environment of greater opportunity than was available to those with whom they were compared. Having decided that genius was inherited, Galton then began to study individual differences in simple sensory and motor functions, since he assumed that these were the functions most closely associated with the constitutional nature of the individual. The value of these sensory and motor tests was questioned, however, as a result of the fact that Galton's statistical method revealed little correlation among the various tests and little relationship with other independent estimates of intelligence, such as teacher's ratings and academic grades.

It was Cattell who brought the idea of the use of tests to America and who coined the term *mental test* (Cattell, 1890). Goddard, an ardent hereditarian, popularized the use of mental tests by employing them in his studies of the feebleminded at the Vineland Training

School. Author of the well-known study of the Kallikak family (Goddard, 1914), he had had long experience with the retarded and was not very optimistic about their educability. What is somewhat difficult to understand is that it was not Galton's or Cattell's tests that Goddard used, but rather the tests of the Binet-Simon scale (Binet and Simon, 1916). Binet had criticized Galton's test as being too simple and too largely sensory and had proposed that the measurement of intelligence would be better accomplished by the measurement of more complex functions such as memory, imagination, and comprehension. He also did not accept the idea of a fixed intelligence, but, on the contrary, believed that intelligence could be modified by experience. The value of the Binet tests lay in the fact that they tended to be relatively successful in differentiating between those who did and did not achieve success in school.

Evidence for the hereditarian viewpoint came from several sources. The first of these was the finding that IQ's of individual children were found to show considerable constancy from childhood to adulthood. This in turn enhanced the confidence in the reliability of the tests. Another bit of circularity. In addition, strong evidence for the hereditary basis of intelligence came from the correlations of IQ scores between people of varying degrees of genetic relationship. Most such studies showed the highest correlation of intelligence scores for identical twins and a decreasing correlation in the following order: fraternal twins, siblings, parents and their children, cousins.

Some of the experimental evidence, however, tends to support the position that the IQ can be modified by environmental experience. Evidence for this view comes from a number of studies of identical twins reared apart. The best known study is that of Newman, Freeman, and Holzinger (1937), who assembled data on nineteen pairs of twins. Some of these twins were separated at six months of age and most of them were separated by at least the end of the second year. The largest difference in IQ found by these investigators was twenty-four points, but less than half of the twins showed a difference of ten points or more. The investigators believed that they were justified in concluding that environmental opportunities accounted for considerable differences in measures of intelligence. However, some critics of the study pointed out the fact that the average difference reported was not substantially greater than the average difference in IQ for identical twins reared together. One of the difficulties involved in the interpretation of such studies is the fact that living apart does not necessarily mean that the twins were subjected to essentially different environmental opportunities.

Additional evidence against the hereditary basis of intelligence comes from studies on IQ constancy. Several investigators studied the correlations between test scores obtained after varying time intervals separating the administrations of the tests. The results obtained show that the correlations, or the stability of position of the individuals within a given group, decrease as the time separating the tests is increased. Furthermore, if the tests are first given at a very early age, the correlations drop even further. Those who believe that the intelligence is fixed discount these findings with the claims that infant tests are unreliable. The nature of the evidence does not permit a definitive resolution of the question.

Similar ambiguities result from the data obtained from longitudinal studies of the variation of intelligence in the same individual. These are necessarily time-consuming because children had to be tested early in life and the retests had to wait for their chronological growth. Goodenough and Maurer (1942) reported changes of from twenty to fifty points in the course of nine years; as they saw no environmental basis for the shifts in IQ, they concluded that the differences might be due to errors of measurement or to inherited patterns of mental growth.

Many workers attempted to separate the effects of nature and nurture by comparing the effects of the nursery school and the orphanage. The orphanage has been assumed to provide an unstimulating environment while the better staffed nursery schools have been assumed to provide the kind of stimulation that might be conducive to intellectual growth. A number of such studies reported increases in the intelligence of the nursery school children that far out-distanced those children who remained in the orphanage (Barrett and Koch, 1930; Skeels et al., 1938; Wooley, 1925). The proponents of the fixed intelligence hypothesis discounted the data because they believed that the studies failed to control all of the relevant factors (McNemar, 1940).

The studies of R. A. Spitz (1945), who attempted to demonstrate the importance of mothering in the first year of life, were impressive. He compared the development of babies in two institutions. In one of these, called "Foundling Home," the babies received very little attention from their mothers after they ceased nursing them at three months of age. In the other institution, called "Nursery," the mothers were permitted to care for and play with their children throughout

the first year. Spitz administered the Hetzer-Wolfe baby tests to the
children and found that the mean Developmental Quotient (DQ)
for the Foundling Home children of 131 at two to three months had
decreased to 72 at ten to twelve months, whereas the mean DQ of the
children in the Nursery group showed a small increase. These differences Spitz attributed to the amount of mothering the children received. The results and conclusions of the study, like those of many
of the other studies, have been severely criticized for inadequate rigor;
and while they are suggestive of some degree of plasticity in the child,
they are not sufficiently clear to demonstrate that intelligence is not a
fixed dimension.

The assumption that intelligence is a fixed dimension has also received much support from those who espoused the doctrine of predetermined development. Behavior is seen as unfolding more or less
automatically as a function of morphological development. For those
who accepted the principle of genetically predetermined development
it seemed natural to include intelligence within the concept. The position received much of its support from Darwin's theory of natural
selection and from the notion that ontogeny recapitulates phylogeny.
According to G. Stanley Hall one can see in the development of each
individual the evolution of the race. Hall's influence was extended by
his pupils, who were prominent in the development of intelligence
tests. Among his students who had an important impact on the field
were H. H. Goddard, F. Kuhlmann, and M. Terman. Arnold Gesell,
who has contributed heavily to the field of child development, was
also a student of Hall. Hall's position regarding behavioral recapitula-
tion was, however, rigid and allowed descriptive norms of behavior at
various ages to serve as explanations of that behavior. No attention
was given to the possibility that maturation was in a large measure
dependent upon the special circumstances of environment of the
developing child.

Thorndike's classical experiments in comparative psychology, using
first chicks in a puzzle box and then cats, dogs, and monkeys, raised
a number of important questions about the growth of intelligence
(Thorndike, 1898). In achieving a solution the animals appeared to
try one thing after another in random fashion until by chance they
performed the act that permitted them to escape from the puzzle box.
These experiments gave rise to a trial and error theory of learning.
Learning was considered to be a matter of strengthening the connection between the stimulus and the response that achieved the goal.
The question of what strengthened the bond between the stimulus

and the correct response was a matter of long dispute and gave rise to two types of explanations. One explanation considered the recency and frequency of the correct response as the critical feature in the learning process. Thorndike himself, however, attempted an explanation by means of the law of effect, which held that the critical feature in the learning process was the consequence of the response; a maladaptive response is weakened and an adaptive response is strengthened. This view is related to Darwin's theory of natural selection; that is, responses, like variations in organisms, survive and persist because they are adaptive. Maturation and learning were seen as essentially distinct processes. The basic response units were dependent upon the maturation of the anatomical structures, which were subsequently arranged in various combinations by stimulus-response bonds built up through experience. The brain was conceived to be somewhat like a telephone switchboard, with the various reflexive responses connected and disconnected within the cerebrum.

The stimulus-response theories of learning were attacked by Gestalt psychologists who considered insight to be the critical feature in problem solution. Köhler's (1925) experiments with chimpanzees led him to the conclusion that there existed an isomorphism between the brain and the stimulus, and that dynamic organizing processes within the brain may result in an insightful solution, which was not dependent upon the gradual strengthening of stimulus-response bonds. The Gestaltist group saw the cerebral organizations underlying insight as coming automatically with the maturation of brain structures, thus giving support to maturation of gene-determined structures and the resultant behavior.

The importance of maturation over learning, and as a consequence of heredity over environment, was given further support by the experimental evidence provided by Coghill. Coghill's study on the larval amblystoma was most illuminating in view of the fact that this amphibian begins life in a transparent egg and can be observed from fertilization to maturity. As a result of his experiments, Coghill says: "Behavior develops from the beginning through the progressive expansion of a perfectly integrated total pattern and the individuation within it of partial patterns which acquire various degrees of discreteness" (Coghill, 1929). He was also able to show that the course of individuation proceeds from head to tail and from central to peripheral structures. It, therefore, became possible to note the parallels between morphological and behavioral development. Coghill's experiments were seen as demonstrating not only that function follows the development of structure, but that the function is innately determined by the structure. The interpretations of Coghill's important study have been criticized as sometimes going beyond the actual observations, but the fact remains that the study gave added empirical evidence for the belief that behavior patterns are genetically determined.

Following Coghill a number of investigators conducted experiments to determine the effects of deprivation or enhancement of specific experiences as compared with control groups, which were allowed the normal full experience of the species. Thus, Carmichael (1926) allowed his control group of salamanders to develop under ordinary conditions while placing an experimental group in chloretone so as to allow for normal cellular growth but no practice in swimming, as the animals became anesthetized. When the control group was swimming about well, the experimental group was removed from the chloretone. As soon as the anesthetic wore off these animals swam as well as the control animals. These findings lent further support to the contention that behavior unfolds automatically as the structures mature.

Mary Shirley (1931) then provided some experiments that suggested that Coghill's developmental principles could be applied to man. She claimed to be able to demonstrate that not only did the head-tailward order of behavior develement take place in children, but also that the order in which various responses appeared in children occurred with a marked consistency. Her findings did not go uncontested. No one denied the orderly development, but Dennis (1960) and others presented evidence to show that the orderly sequences of motor development were probably a function of both genetic influences common to the species and the typical sequences of experience that come with growing up in a human family. Other experimenters, including Birch (1945), have shown that deprivations of experience have much to do with the rate at which behavior develops in a given organism. In the light of these experiments it is probably more realistic to consider explanations based upon continuous environmental-organism interactions. Even if one accepts the evidence that the intellectual capacity of an individual is, to a large degree, genetically predetermined, it is still necessary to inquire as to the extent to which this capacity is influenced by or dependent upon experience or environmental influence.

Studies of central nervous system function constitute another approach to the question of the origin of intelligent behavior. The conception that behavior develops through stimulus-response chaining implied a brain hooked up like a switchboard. But increasing evidence was accumulated that could not be subsumed under that type of central nervous system. Hunter (1912, 1924) took the position that in animals high on the phyletic scale some kind of symbolic process was in evidence. He inferred this from his observation that children and chimpanzees were able to use the cues for the location of food even after substantial delays between seeing the cues and approaching the food. His double-alternation problems, in which spatial and kinesthetic cues were eliminated, were also designed to study symbolic processes. While rats could not learn a double alternation, cats and dogs could; and chimpanzees and children could not only learn such a series but could generalize it to a new series. He was, therefore, inclined to the position that some responses of the organism come to have symbolic value in the learning process. From these and similar experiments, many investigators concluded that the central process involved must be something more than a switchboard connection between afferent and efferent events. Both the Gestaltists and Lashley placed much importance on central processes without stressing the role of experience.

In contrast the work of Harlow (1949) shows that experience plays a major role in problem solution. In his investigations of "learning to learn" in monkeys, Harlow started with object-quality discriminations that required a choice to be made between one of two objects which differed in a specific attribute. He then presented the more complicated oddity problems. In these oddity experiments both position and perceptual characteristics of the objects were rewarded ambiguously, and only the odd object was regularly rewarded. As a result, no specific perceptual cues were available to the animals, as they were required to select the object that was unlike the other two, which were identical. In some of his later experiments, he was able to demonstrate that his animals could perform according to two originally antagonistic learning sets with a minimum of interference.

Harlow's findings were not inconsistent with the notion that heredity sets limits upon the potential of an organism, but they did tend to indicate that the "learning set" might make insight possible, that these learning sets do not come ready-made, but must be acquired, and that once acquired they increase the capacity of the organism to solve certain kinds of problems.

It was Hebb (1949), however, who made the greatest impact on the problem by bringing together the findings in neurophysiology and psychology so as to provide for a better understanding of the role of central processes in perception and problem-solving. He distinguished between primary (first) learning and later learning in the human being. The slow primary learning is accounted for by the large association areas in the human brain relative to the size of the sensory projection areas. For learning to occur it is necessary to establish "control of association-area activity by sensory events" (Hebb, 1949, p. 123). The larger the association areas the longer it takes to establish control by a given sensory area. To give this notion a quantitative expression Hebb speaks of the A/S ratio (A refers to association areas and S to sensory projection areas). He cites experimental evidence regarding phylogenetic changes in learning capacity, which he summarizes as follows: "(1) more complex relationships can be learned by higher species (with large A/S ratios) at maturity; (2) simple relationships are learned about as promptly by lower as by higher species; (3) the first learning is *slower* in higher than in lower species" (Hebb, 1949, p. 116). The activity of the association areas is the result of the innate intrinsic activity present at birth, upon which is imposed an organization attributable to sensory inputs.

Hebb's notion of the important role of central processes in behavior suggested that intelligence would probably be a function of the variegation and mobility of the cell assemblies established through primary learning within those regions of the brain not immediately concerned with receptor inputs or motor outputs. This conception suggested further that adult intelligence should vary with opportunities for perceptual and perhaps even motor experience early in life. As a consequence of this view a number of studies concerned with the effects of infantile experiences on later learning and problem-solving were conducted. These studies have shown that rats reared with ample opportunities for a variety of perceptual experience learned mazes more readily than rats reared with minimal perceptual experience. Pet-reared rats with a background of highly varied experience have been found to perform with more facility on the Hebb-Williams test of intelligence than did cage-reared rats with a background of little variation in experience. Similarly, Thompson and Heron (1954) have shown that in a wide variety of situations pet-reared dogs behaved in a fashion much more intelligent than their litter-mates who were cage-reared for the first eight months of their lives. Early experiences have a more profound effect on adult intelligence of dogs than rats. This is consonant with the expectation that the importance of infantile experiences for later intelligence is a function of the size of the A/S ratio.

Further development in the theorizing about brain function has come from those who are interested in the programming of electronic computers for problem-solving. Newell, Shaw, and Simon (1958), for example, have postulated that the phenomena of set and insight and the hierarchical structure of the response system are consequences of an active organization of the central processes. In contrast to a passive electro-chemical system (or passive switchboard) they have postulated an information-processing system with large storage capacity for complex strategies (programs) that may be evoked by stimuli. The content of these strategies is largely determined by previous experiences of the system. The learning sets of Harlow's animals have been viewed as resembling the strategies for the processing of information wired into electric computers. The strategies are assumed to be stored in those regions of the brain that receive no receptor inputs and have no direct access to musculature. The investigators have described the operation of the central hierarchical systems in such a way as to indicate that for them intelligence would consist of the strategies for processing information that have been differentiated and are available for operation in a variety of situations.

A discussion of intelligence would not be complete without mention of the important contributions of Piaget. Piaget's studies (1954) led him to see life as a continuous creative interaction between the organism and the environment. He distinguished between inner organization and outer adaptation. He postulated two complementary processes, which he called assimilation and accommodation. When the organism makes use of something from the environment and in addition incorporates it, the process is called assimilation. Thus, whenever the organism sees something new in terms of something familiar, or acts in a new situation as it has acted in the past, assimilation is in operation. Assimilation results in the building up of internal structures, analogous to the Gestalt structures. Accommodation occurs when a stimulus evokes not merely a fixed response, but simultaneously modifies the elicited response pattern. The epigenesis of the mind is seen as a process that transforms the reflexive schemata of the newborn infant progressively through differentiations to the logical organization of adult intelligence.

Piaget has been careful to note that the appearance of the behavior depends on the continuous interplay of internal structures with the environment. The rapidity of the child's rate of intellectual growth is seen as related directly to the stimulating situations to which he must accommodate. Piaget's experiments present a strong case for the position that the continuous organism-environment interaction produces a gradualness of change in structure.

Concluding Remarks. There remain many unanswered questions about the nature and origin of intelligence, but the present evidence at least indicates that the problem cannot be reduced simply to the relative importance of heredity and environment. The fact remains that it is impossible to discuss heredity except in terms of environment, or environment except in terms of heredity. Only the phenotype can be measured, and to determine the extent to which the genotype can be modified by environment would require submitting that genotype to every possible environmental experience.

The fact that original endowment sets some limits beyond which the individual may not go, no matter how favorable the environment experienced, cannot be doubted. We do not know the extent to which the intelligence may be improved, but there appears to be considerable evidence that improving the match between the demands of the environment and the child's capacity to accommodate might serve to enhance the rate of development and ultimately result in increased capacity (Hunt, 1961).

Those who deal in a professional way with the developing child should not be satisfied with the various scales that purport to give norms of accomplishment at any particular month of chronological age. Attention should be given to the kind and variety of experience to which the child has been exposed, and the possibility of improvement as a consequence of enhancement of stimulation should not be overlooked.

It is true, of course, that the effectiveness of interventions will be dependent upon the discovery of the kind of environments conducive to intellectual development. This is a tremendous undertaking; and even if the facts become known, it would also be necessary to discover ways of enabling the parents and others to provide the necessary stimulation and environment to the growing child. Finally, for full development, the important environmental encounters must provide pleasure and stimulate interest and curiosity to propel the individual toward the realization of his full potential.

REFERENCES

ALEXANDER, W. P. Intelligence concrete and abstract. *Brit. J. Psychol.,* 1935, Monograph Suppl. XIX.

BARRETT, H. E., & KOCH, H. L. The effect of nursery school training upon the mental test performance of a group of orphanage children. *J. genet. Psychol.*, 1930, **37**, 102–122.

BINET, A. Nouvelles recherches sur la mesure du niveau intellectuel chez les enfants. *Année Psychologique,* 1908, **14**, 1–94.

BINET, A., & SIMON, T. *The development of intelligence in children.* Transl. E. S. Kite. Publications of the Training School at Vineland, No. 11, 1916.

BIRCH, H. G. The relation of previous experience to insightful problem-solving. *J. comp. Psychol.,* 1945, **38**, 367–383.

CARMICHAEL, L. The development of behavior in vertebrates experimentally removed from influence of external stimulation. *Psychol. Rev.,* 1926, **33**, 51–58.

CATTELL, J. McK. Mental tests and measurements. *Mind,* 1890, **15**, 373–380.

COGHILL, C. E. *Anatomy and the problem of behavior.* New York: Macmillan, 1929.

DENNIS, W. Causes of retardation among institutional children. *J. genet. Psychol.,* 1960, **96**, 47–59.

EBBINGHAUS, H. Uber eine neue methode zur Prüfung geistiger Fähigkeiten und ihre Anwendung bei Schuldkindern. *Zeitschrift für Psychologie und Physiologie der Sinnesorgane,* 1897, **13**, 401.

FREEMAN, F. D. *Mental tests.* New York: Houghton Mifflin, 1926.

GALTON, F. *Hereditary genius: an inquiry into its laws and consequences.* London: Macmillan, 1869.

GODDARD, H. H. *The Kallikak family.* New York: Macmillan, 1914.

GOODENOUGH, FLORENCE L., & MAURER, KATHERINE M. *The mental growth of children from two to fourteen years: a study of the predictive value of the Minnesota Pre-school Scales.* Minneapolis: Univer. of Minnesota Press, 1942.

HARLOW, H. F. The formation of learning sets. *Psychol. Rev.,* 1949, **56**, 51–65.

HART, B., & SPEARMAN, C. General ability, its existence and nature. *Brit. J. Psychol.,* 1912–13, **5**, 51–84.

HEBB, D. O. *The organization of behavior.* New York: Wiley, 1949.

HUNT, J. McV. *Intelligence and experience.* New York: Ronald Press, 1961.

HUNTER, W. S. The delayed reactions in animals and children. *Behav. Monogr.,* 1912, Vol. 2, No. 1, Serial No. 6.

———. The symbolic process. *Psychol. Rev.,* 1924, **31**, 478–497.

KÖHLER, W. *The mentality of apes.* New York: Harcourt, Brace, & World, 1925.

McNEMAR, Q. A critical examination of the University of Iowa studies of environmental influences upon the I.Q. *Psychol. Bull.,* 1940, **37**, 63–92.

NEWALL, A., SHAW, J. C., & SIMON, H. A. Elements of a theory of human problem solving. *Psychol. Rev.,* 1958, **65**, 151–166.

NEWMAN, H. H., FREEMAN, F. N., & HOLZINGER, K. J. *Twins: a study of heredity and environment.* Chicago: Univer. of Chicago Press, 1937.

PIAGET, J. *The construction of reality in the child.* (Transl. Margaret Cook.) New York: Basic Books, 1954.

SHIRLEY, MARY M. A motor sequence favors the maturation theory. *Psychol. Bull.,* 1931, **28**, 204–205.

SKEELS, H. M., UPDEGRAFF, R., WELLMAN, B. L., & WILLIAMS, H. M. A study of environmental stimulation: an orphanage preschool project. *Univer. Iowa Stud. Child Welf.*, 1938, **15**, No. 4.

SPEARMAN, C. *Abilities of man.* London: Macmillan, 1932.

SPITZ, R. A. Hospitalism: an inquiry into the genesis of psychiatric conditions in early childhood. *Psychoanal. Stud. Child,* 1945,**1**, 53–74.

STERN, W. *The psychological methods of testing intelligence.* Baltimore: Warwick & York, 1914.

THOMPSON, W. R., & HERON, W. The effects of restricting early experience on the problem solving capacity of dogs. *Canad. J. Psychol.,* 1954, **8**, 17–31.

THORNDIKE, E. L. Animal intelligence. *Psychol. Rev., Monogr. Suppl.,* 1898, Vol. 2, No. 4.

———. *Educational psychology.* New York: Teacher's College, Columbia Univer., 1913–14.

THORNDIKE, E. L., BREGMAN, E. O., COBB, M. V., WOODYARD, E., *et al. The measurement of intelligence.* New York: New York Bureau of Publications, Teacher's College, Columbia Univ., 1927.

THURSTONE, L. L. Theory of attitude measurement. *Psychol. Rev.,* 1929, **36**, 222–241.

WECHSLER, D. Cognitive, conative, and non-intellective intelligence. *Amer. Psychol.,* 1950, **5**, 78–83.

———. *The measurement of adult intelligence.* (3d ed.) Baltimore: Williams and Wilkins, 1944.

WOOLEY, H. T. The validity of standards of mental measurement in young childhood. *School and Soc.,* 1925, **21**, 476–482.

3

PERINATAL FACTORS
AND INTELLIGENCE

Janet B. Hardy

The subject matter encompassed by this title is wide in scope, complex in nature, and at best incompletely understood. A brief general discussion of some of the biologic factors that may modify intelligence will be presened in an attempt to establish a frame of reference for more detailed discussion of a limited number of specific conditions that may be operative during the perinatal period.

Definition of terms may be necessary. The perinatal period is the time span from conception to the end of the neonatal period. The neonatal period begins with birth and terminates with the twenty-eighth day of postnatal life. The paranatal period is the period immediately surrounding birth.

Some of the data to be discussed later involve preliminary information coming from the Collaborative Project on Cerebral Palsy, Mental Retardation, and Allied Neurologic Defects in Children (more recently named the Collaborative Perinatal Project). The Collaborative Project is a prospective, multi-disciplinary study of some 50,000 pregnancies, with follow-up of the surviving children to school age. This study is being carried out in 14 medical institutions across the country. It is sponsored and co-ordinated by the National Institute of Neurological Diseases and Blindness. Its objective is the identification of factors that may adversely affect the mother or the pregnancy, resulting in fetal loss or in the continuum of fetal loss represented by

JANET B. HARDY, M.D., is associate professor of pediatrics, The Johns Hopkins University School of Medicine.

such handicapping conditions as cerebral palsy, mental retardation, blindness, epilepsy, and problems in communication.

The Collaborative Perinatal Project has enrolled pregnant women as they appeared for obstetric care. Since 1959 approximately 35,000 women have been included in the study as a whole, and about 3,200 in the Johns Hopkins Project. Data are being collected in the following areas.

1. Family background: parental age, race, education, socio-economic status, occupation, genetic background.

2. Gravida's past history: medical, gynecologic, and obstetric.

3. Events during the current pregnancy: maternal illness, particularly virus infections, cigarette smoking, work history, complications of pregnancy.

4. Events occurring during labor and leading to delivery. Particular attention is paid to the fetal heart rate, presence of meconium, and other evidence of fetal distress.

5. Laboratory studies: maternal and fetal blood grouping and Coombs' test (for the identification of possible blood group incompatibility and isoimmunization), virus studies of maternal and fetal serum, placental pathology, pathologic study of fetal losses including neuropathology.

6. The immediate condition of the neonate: Apgar score [1] at one, two, and five minutes after complete delivery, birth weight, physical status, and any procedures required to effect resuscitation.

7. The nursery course of the neonate: routine pediatric examinations, neurologic evaluation, bilirubin and hematocrit determinations centered around 48 hours of age. Medications, oxygen therapy, other procedures, and laboratory work are noted. A diagnostic summary is completed at discharge.

8. Follow-up examinations are carried out as follows on the surviving children:

Age	*Type of Examination*
4 months	Pediatric
8 months	Psychologic
12 months	Neurologic
24 months	Pediatric
36 months	Language, hearing, and speech
48 months	Psychologic

[1] The Apgar score is derived from observation of five parameters. Heart rate, respiratory effort, color, reflex irritability, and muscle tone are each rated on a scale from 0 to 2. A score of 10 is optimal, scores of 6 or less signify increasing degrees of fetal depression (Apgar, 1958) .

An interval medical history is taken at each follow-up visit and at six-month intervals between visits. Further neurologic, speech and hearing, and psychometric evaluations are planned for age seven to eight years.

Of the several objectives to which these examinations are addressed, I propose to discuss one: the relationship between perinatal factors and defective intelligence. Although another chapter in this book is devoted to a discussion of the nature of intelligence, it is still necessary to submit here a brief working definition which has guided us in the selection of testing instruments and the formulation of conclusions. Intelligence is viewed as the functional expression of a complex, highly integrated series of component parts, including on the input side perception (auditory, visual, and tactile); the ability to identify, process, store, and recall stimuli received; the ability to select among the stimuli received and to activate the output side of the system. Included in our definition of intelligence is the ability to learn. Learning itself is a complex process and is dependent not only on suitable opportunity on the one hand, and intact neural circuitry on the other hand, but also upon a variety of psychologic factors, such as motivation, attention span, and freedom from interference by emotional problems.

We adopt the view expounded by Hunt in his provocative book, *Intelligence and Experience* (1961), that intelligence is not fixed and immutable, but is, rather, to use his terms, a set of "central structures" developed in the course of child-environment interaction (including intrauterine environment). The role of heredity consists of setting limits to development.

An evaluation of the possible effects of various biologic factors on intelligence must be based upon the expected distribution of intelligence in the population. This is shown in Figure 1, from Penrose's book, *The Biology of Mental Defect* (1963). The distribution follows in the main a Gaussian curve with approximately 90 per cent of the population falling within two standard deviations of the mean. The curve is, however, actually skewed to the left because there is a larger number of individuals at the lower end of the intellectual scale than would be expected on a purely theoretical basis.

We now come to a discussion of mental retardation. Table 1 gives a breakdown of some etiologic factors involved in retarded intellectual development. It is a modification of the table presented in Harper's book, *Preventive Pediatrics* (1962). Table 2 is concerned with the timing of critical events related to retarded mental development.

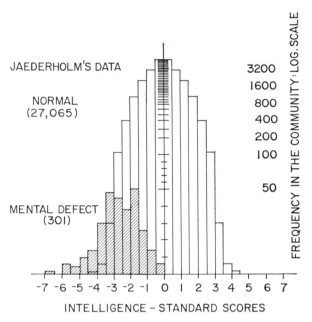

F$_{IG.}$ 1: Theoretical distribution of intelligence. Estimate based on Binet test scores of 301 defective and 261 normal children. (Modified from Penrose, 1963.)

FAMILIAL OR CULTURAL RETARDATION

Familial, or cultural retardation is the term used to describe the condition of those individuals falling into the group of the mildly retarded, usually in the IQ range of 60 to 80 points, for whom no immediate etiologic factor is discernible. Those individuals, who according to Harper (1962) account for between 65 to 75 per cent of all retarded persons, are found for the most part in low socio-economic and culturally poor environments. While the relative etiologic roles of the genetic, perinatal, and later environmental factors in this important group are unclear, there seems to be good reason to believe that socio-cultural factors may be of great importance. Further discussion of this aspect of retardation is beyond the scope of this presentation.

GENETIC DETERMINANTS OF RETARDATION

The genetic determinants of intelligence are complex and presumably quite numerous. In trying to assign an etiologic basis to a case of mental retardation one must make a judgment as to whether the

TABLE 1:   Etiologic Classification of Mental Retardation

I.   *Familial* or Cultural Retardation (relative roles of nature and nurture unclear)

II. *Genetic*
  A. Pathologic or mutant genes
    1. Metabolic defects—PKU, galactosemia, cerebral degenerative disease, etc.
    2. Cellular dysplasia—Sturge Weber, neurofibromatosis, tuberous sclerosis, etc.
    3. Cerebral defect plus malformation of skull—microcephaly, craniostenosis, hypertelorism, etc.
    4. Hereditary mental retardation—unclassified
  B. Chromosomal abnormalities—usually nondisjunction and translocation
    1. Mongolism
    2. Turner's syndrome, Klinefelter's syndrome
    3. Other types

III. *Acquired*
  A. Prenatal influences
    1. Demographic—maternal race, age, socio economic status
    2. Infections—rubella, toxoplasmosis, cytomegalic disease, syphilis, and urinary tract infections which may lead to premature delivery
    3. Multiple pregnancy
    4. Physical agents—irradiation
    5. Isoimmunization—particularly blood group incompatibility
    6. Hormonal—hypothyroidism
    7. Chronic nutritional deficit—placental insufficiency syndrome
    8. Drugs
        a. Those with teratogenic properties
        b. Those which interfere with bilirubin metabolism
  B. Paranatal influences (high incidence of premature delivery)
    1. Asphyxia—impaired fetal blood supply due to prolapse cord, abruptio placentae
    2. Trauma
        a. Mechanical—cerebral birth injury
        b. Biochemical—anoxia with acidosis, hyperbilirubinemia, hypoglycemia, hypernatremia
  C. Postnatal
    1. Infection—diarrhea, meningitis, encephalitis
    2. Trauma
    3. Poisoning
    4. Postimmunization encephalitis
    5. Psychosis with mental retardation

IV. *Unknown*—high incidence of maternal bleeding, toxemia, and prematurity

---

SOURCE: Harper, 1959.

TABLE 2:   Timing of Possible Causes of Mental Defect

Usual Terminology		Epoch	Agent
A. Genetic, hereditary, endogenous, due to nature	(*i*)	Remote	Spontaneous mutation in ancestral germ cells
	(*ii*)	Recent	Spontaneous or induced mutation; meiotic errors in parental germ cells
B. Environmental, exogenous, due to nurture	(*i*)	Early prenatal	Injury to the fertilized ovum during early stages of development; maternal disease
	(*ii*)	Late prenatal	Intrauterine disease; mal-nutrition, infection, incom-patibility
	(*iii*)	Intranatal	Abnormal birth
	(*iv*)	Postnatal	Diseases or accidents in infancy or childhood; un-favorable social environ-ments

SOURCE: Penrose, 1963.

affected individual is beyond the expected pattern of intelligence for his family. This may not be easy. Benda (1952) has provided a useful rule-of-thumb for this purpose. He points out that in respect to intelligence the children can be expected to fall within a range which extends from two standard deviations above the brighter parent to two standard deviations below the duller parent. For example, if one considers two parents with IQ's of 130 and 125 respectively, the expected range for their children would extend from 160 IQ at the upper limit to 95 at the lower (assuming a standard deviation of 15). If, on the other hand, one considers a parental pair with IQ's of 85 and 75 (which is borderline defective), the expected IQ range for the children would be from 115, which is high average, down to 45, which is frankly defective. When one comes to consider the possible etiologic significance of an isolated antecedent event such as paranatal anoxia, or hyperbilirubinemia, the possible effect must be considered in rela-tion to the range of intellectual function to be expected on a purely genetic basis for the individual.

The genetic determinants of mental retardation can be divided into two general categories, one due to mutant genes and the other to abnormal chromosomes. It is estimated that together these account for 15 to 20 per cent of retarded individuals. Phenylketonuria and galactosemia are good examples of genetic metabolic defects due to mutant genes. When untreated these conditions result in severe degrees of mental retardation. The categories produced by abnormalities of the chromosomes may involve many gene loci. Two major types of chromosomal abnormality are recognized. The more frequent, termed nondisjunction, results in an abnormal number of chromosomes as a consequence of a failure of equal meiotic division during the formation of either the ovum or the sperm. Nondisjunction, which occurs with increased frequency toward the end of the reproductive period, is the basic defect in most, but not all, cases of Mongolism. The markedly increased incidence of Mongolism in the children of women becoming pregnant at 40 years of age and over is undoubtedly due to this factor. Nondisjunction is also responsible for Klinefelter's and Turner's syndromes, both of which, like Mongolism, may be accompanied by mental retardation.

ACQUIRED FACTORS

It was as long ago as 1862 that Little, a British obstetrician, published a series of papers clearly relating poor neurologic outcome in the child (cerebral palsy and mental retardation) to certain pregnancy factors, particularly trauma and hypoxia during delivery. However, it is to the paper of Lilienfeld and Parkhurst published in 1951 that we are indebted for the useful concept of "the continuum of reproductive wastage." They pointed out that certain factors, when present during pregnancy at the proper time and in sufficient dosage, cause fetal death. However, if operative at a less optimal time in embryonic development, or in sublethal dosage, these factors, while not sufficient to cause death, may result in handicapping conditions such as cerebral palsy, mental retardation, epilepsy, and blindness. This thesis has been supported by a number of epidemiologic studies (Eastman et al., 1962; Lilienfeld, Pasamanick, and Rogers, 1955), from which has come information about certain events during pregnancy associated with a continuum of handicap in the surviving offspring.

The concept of minimal brain injury as a consequence of perinatal insult is not a new one, but it is only in recent years that widespread attention has focused on the possible role of perinatal factors, such as minimal brain injury, in the etiology of cognitive and behavioral difficulties recognized later in childhood (Graham et al., 1962;

Knobloch and Pasamanick, 1959; Lilienfeld, Pasamanick, and Rogers, 1955; Paine, 1962; Prechtl and Stemmer, 1962). A recent study by Klatskin (1964) of two groups of three-year-old children, one of average intelligence and the other of superior intelligence, suggests that isolated failures on standard intelligence tests, particularly tasks involving complex patterns and language integration, can be correlated with stressful perinatal experiences, such as maternal toxemia, intrapartum hemorrhage, difficult delivery, and fetal hypoxia.

Prenatal Influences. There is evidence that Negro and other non-white children have a higher incidence of neurologic difficulty and mental retardation than Caucasians. Presumably, this is at least in part the result of such perinatal influences as the incidence of premature delivery, which is higher in the non-white groups. It has been shown by Rider, Tayback, and Knobloch (1955) in Baltimore, Stewart (1955) in England, and others that social factors, such as socio-economic status and occupation, play a role in the incidence of premature birth. There is an inverse relationship between socio-economic level and the incidence of premature delivery.

Maternal age is also an important factor in determining the likelihood of premature delivery. Battaglia, Frazier, and Hellegers (1963) have published results of a study on approximately 750 juvenile patients followed in the Woman's Clinic of the Johns Hopkins Hospital. These girls were fourteen years of age or less at the time they became pregnant. They had an incidence of premature delivery of 23 per cent as compared with 16 per cent in the next higher age bracket (fifteen through nineteen years). The incidence of prematurity for the Negro clinic patients as a whole at the Johns Hopkins Hospital was approximately 13 per cent and for white clinic patients 8 per cent, while for white private patients it was about 4.8 per cent. In addition to the increased risk of prematurity in the offspring of young mothers, there is also a higher incidence of perinatal mortality among them.

Our Hopkins Collaborative Project data are consistent with other findings, as they suggest enhanced fetal difficulty for the babies of young mothers. Not only have several of these babies died during the early months after hospital discharge but the expectation for their mental development appears to be less favorable than is the case for our Collaborative Project population as a whole. The mean Binet IQ at age four years was eighty-seven for a group of twenty-eight Negro children (one slightly premature) whose mothers were under sixteen years at the time of pregnancy, as compared with a mean IQ of ninety-three for the total Negro group tested. For the white children whose mothers were under sixteen the mean Binet IQ was ninety-three as compared with ninety-seven for the total white group.

The most favorable maternal age range with respect to perinatal mortality and morbidity is from twenty to thirty-five years. There is an increased perinatal mortality among infants of older mothers, and the findings of the Collaborative Project confirm this. The number of four-year-old children in our sample whose mothers were over thirty-five years of age is still too small to permit evaluation of the long-range effect of advanced maternal age on intellectual development.

Following the list of prenatal influences brings us to a consideration of maternal infection during pregnancy. The fact that certain virus diseases can cause a variety of congenital malformations in the fetus was clearly established with respect to rubella by the memorable observations of Gregg (1945), following a serious and widespread outbreak of rubella in Australia. As the children conceived shortly before the outbreak of rubella came to school age, a wide spectrum of defect, including microcephaly, microphthalmia, cataracts, mental retardation, hearing loss, and cardiac and dental defects, were related to maternal infection during the first trimester of pregnancy. The incidence of congenital malformation has been estimated to be as high as 80 per cent of offspring.

In the United States estimates of the incidence of congenital malformation following rubella have been for the most part much lower (Greenberg, Pellitteri, and Barton, 1957). The best available figures appear to be those of Michaels and Mellin (1960), which suggest that maternal rubella during the first four weeks of pregnancy carries a risk that 47 per cent of the fetuses will be malformed; in the second four weeks the risk is 22 per cent; and in the third four week period it is 7 per cent; after the first trimester the rate of malformation was no longer elevated. Present experience may modify these figures.

Much of the difficulty in interpreting the results of studies of rubella infection during pregnancy has stemmed from the fact that the diagnosis of rubella was made on a clinical basis and subject to confusion with several other virus infections associated with rash, such as infection with Coxachi 9 and Echo 9, to mention only two. The isolation of the rubella virus by Weller and Neva (1962) and Parkman, Buescher, and Artenstein (1962), and the opportunity to study a more recent outbreak of rubella in this country, should make possible more definitive estimates of the risks involved. Serologic studies on some 20,000 pregnant women in the Collaborative Project show that approximately 18 per cent are theoretically at risk of infection, 82 per cent having demonstrable rubella antibodies in the serum (Sever, Schiff, and Huebner, 1963).

There is evidence that prenatal infection with the virus of cytomegalic inclusion disease (salivary gland virus) may cause severe congenital malformation. Its damaging effect as a neonatal infection has also been well documented (Medearis, 1964; Rowe, 1960).

Toxoplasmosis is a widely endemic protozoan infection, usually subclinical in adults. It has been recognized as a cause of abortion; the severe clinical forms recognized in the neonate are known to be associated with eye lesions, intracranial calcification, and severe degrees of mental retardation.

Syphilis, which in the past carried a high incidence of congenital infection and was believed to be a potent cause of malformation, is now rarely seen and is of negligible importance in this respect.

Infections of the urinary tract during pregnancy are mentioned because of the demonstration by Kass (1961) and Henderson, Entwisle, and Tayback (1961) of the increased rate of premature delivery, and of perinatal mortality and morbidity, among the babies of women with both clinical and subclinical infection of the urinary tract.

Multiple pregnancy has an established relationship with mental retardation (Berg and Kerman, 1960; Drillien, 1961). Eastman *et al.* (1962) in their retrospective study of 753 cerebrally palsied and 759 presumably normal children in New York showed that the incidence of twin pregnancy was 7.4 per cent in the cerebrally palsied group as compared with 1.3 per cent in the control group. The incidence of prematurity among the infants resulting from the twin pregnancies was 72.2 per cent in the cerebral palsy group as compared with 56.6 per cent in the controls. Aside from prematurity, fetal insult in twins may be due to the high incidence of breech delivery in the second twin, with its increased risk of trauma and hypoxia. It appears, therefore, that the association between multiple pregnancy and retarded mental development is due primarily to the increased incidence of prematurity, trauma, and anoxia, rather than the fact of multiple birth. A more detailed discussion of this point is given under the heading of *Paranatal Influences.*

Maternal isoimmunization as the result of blood group incompatibility between mother and fetus, particularly with Rh factor, has long been recognized as an etiologic factor in kernicterus. This condition is characterized in its severe forms by cerebral palsy, usually of the dyskinesic or athetoid type, mental retardation, and hearing loss. Kernicterus occurs because of the neurotoxic effect of the high levels of serum bilirubin, brought about in this instance by the hemolysis of fetal red blood cells coated by the maternal antibody resulting from isoimmunization. This point is discussed further under hyperbilirubinemia. In the subjects studied by Eastman *et al.* (1962) the incidence of hemolytic disease in the cerebral palsy group was 5.8 per cent (40/689), as compared with 0.3 per cent (2/695) in the control series. All 40 cases of cerebral palsy with hemolytic disease were dyskinesic in type, and made up about one-fifth of the total group of dyskinesics.

The importance of hormonal control of pregnancy should not be minimized. Habitual abortion and premature delivery frequently result from inadequate hormonal support during pregnancy, particularly in respect to the thyroid and corpus luteal hormones. Adequate levels of thyroid hormone are essential to the rapidly developing fetal nervous system, both during intrauterine life and in the early months of postnatal life. The severe degrees of mental retardation associated with the athyroid and hypothyroid states are well known (cretinism).

Paranatal Influences. A number of different conditions occurring either singly or in combinations about the time of birth may result in fetal death or injury. Premature birth, particularly where the infant weighs less than 1,500 gms. (3.3 lbs.), carries a high risk of neonatal mortality, and of handicap in the surviving child. As may be seen from Table 1, the factors associated with prematurity are asphyxia (hypoxia), and trauma, which may be either gross mechanical trauma during delivery or cellular trauma resulting from biochemical abnormalities. The biochemical abnormalities, such as hypoxia with metabolic acidosis, hyperbilirubinemia, and hyperelectrolytemia, are all of more frequent occurrence in the small premature infant than in the mature infant, and may be in large part responsible for the poor outcome observed in many small infants.

The most clear-cut etiologic factors in fetal anoxia are abruptio placentae and prolapse of the umbilical cord. Other possible causes are hypertensive toxemia of pregnancy and postmaturity. In the series of Eastman *et al.* (1962) abruptio placentae was encountered in 3.9 per cent (27/689) of the cases resulting in cerebral palsy as compared with 1.3 per cent (9/695) of the controls; prolapse of the cord was present in 2.8 per cent (18/689) of the cerebral palsy series in contrast with 0.3 per cent (2/695) of the controls. These differences are statistically significant, as is the difference in the rate of toxemia of pregnancy which was encountered in 4.7 per cent (32/689) of the gravida in the cerebral palsy series as compared with 2.2 per cent (15/695) of the controls. Postmaturity and prolonged labor were both encountered with somewhat increased frequency in the pregnancies in the cerebral palsy group as compared with the controls, but the difference was not significant. The extensive pathologic studies of Courville (1952 and 1959) and the beautifully conducted experimental studies of Windle, Becker, and Weil (1944) document the fact that hypoxia is an important cause of necrosis of cerebral tissue leading to abnormal neuropsychiatric manifestations, including cerebral palsy.

The Apgar score, mentioned earlier, can be considered a useful index of fetal hypoxia at or after delivery. It must be remembered, however, that low scores may result from the depressant effects of maternal oversedation and/or anesthesia, as well as from the depressant effects of trauma to the fetus. Because the anesthetic effects are usually transitory, the five-minute Apgar score has a higher correlation with fetal injury, neonatal mortality, and subsequent evidence of neurologic abnormality than the one-minute Apgar score, as shown in Figure 2. This graph is from preliminary data compiled by Ken-

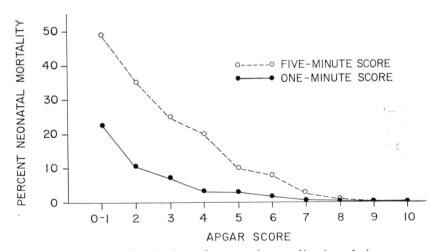

Fig. 2: Per cent distribution of neonatal mortality in relation to one-minute and five-minute Apgar scores. Preliminary data from the Collaborative Perinatal Project compiled by Kennedy, Drage, and Schwartz (1963).

nedy, Drage, and Schwartz (1963) on approximately 10,000 cases in the Collaborative Perinatal Project. As may be seen in the graph, babies with Apgar scores of 7 and above have little risk of neonatal death. A sharp increase in mortality was encountered with five-minute scores of 5 and below, and with one-minute scores of 2 and below.

Tables 3, 4, and 5 show findings on gait, muscle tone, and neurologic status, respectively, at the one-year neurologic examination in children grouped according to the five-minute Apgar score. A progressive increase in the rate of abnormality encountered is seen as the Apgar score decreases from 9–10, through 7–8, 4–6, to 0–3.

TABLE 3: Abnormalities of Gait and Posture at One Year as a Function of the Five-Minute Apgar Score

Abnormalities of Gait and Posture	Five-Minute Score									
	0–3		4–6		7–8		9–10		Totals	
	No.	%	No.	%	No.	%	No.	%	No.	%
Present	10	16.9	26	13.5	42	7.7	301	6.0	379	6.5
Absent	49	83.1	167	86.5	504	92.3	4,717	94.0	5,437	93.5
Total	59	100.0	193	100.0	546	100.0	5,018	100.0	5,816	100.0

SOURCE: Preliminary data, the Collaborative Perinatal Project, compiled by Kennedy, Drage, and Schwartz (1963).

TABLE 4: Abnormalities of Muscle Tone at One Year as a Function of the Five-Minute Apgar Score

Abnormalities of Tone	Five-Minute Score									
	0–3		4–6		7–8		9–10		Totals	
	No.	%	No.	%	No.	%	No.	%	No.	%
Abnormal [a]	8	13.6	11	5.7	22	4.0	176	3.5	217	3.7
Normal	51	86.4	183	94.3	531	96.0	4,873	96.5	5,638	96.3
Total	59	100.0	194	100.0	553	100.0	5,049	100.0	5,855	100.0

[a] Includes hypotonic, hypertonic, and combination of both.

SOURCE: Preliminary data, the Collaborative Perinatal Project, compiled by Kennedy, Drage, and Schwartz (1963).

TABLE 5: Neurologic Status at One Year as a Function of the Five-Minute Apgar Score

One-Year Neurologic Findings	Five-Minute Score								Totals	
	0–3		4–6		7–8		9–10			
	No.	%	No.	%	No.	%	No.	%	No.	%
Abnormal	9	8.0	18	5.3	33	3.0	135	1.6	195	2.0
Suspect	13	11.5	30	8.8	87	7.9	562	6.8	692	7.1
Normal	91	80.5	292	85.9	983	89.1	7,531	91.6	8,897	90.9
Total	113	100.0	340	100.0	1,103	100.0	8,228	100.0	9,784	100.0

SOURCE: Preliminary data, the Collaborative Perinatal Project, compiled by Kennedy, Drage, and Schwartz (1963).

We turn now to the possible toxic effect of hyperbilirubinemia and the relationship of elevated serum bilirubin levels during the neonatal period to the risk of subsequent neurologic and/or developmental defects in the child. The relationship between hyperbilirubinemia and kernicterus has long been appreciated. Hemolysis on the basis of isoimmunization due to maternal-fetal blood group incompatibility accounts for no more than half of cases of hyperbilirubinemia in our infants; other causes are infection, immaturity of liver function, and unknown factors. High levels of serum bilirubin may be toxic regardless of the cause; and for the past fifteen years exchange transfusion to "wash out" the excess bilirubin has been fairly standard pediatric practice when the serum bilirubin level has reached 20–25 mg.% (i.e., 20–25 mg. per 100 cc. serum).

In order to determine the relationship between hyperbilirubinemia during the neonatal period and subsequent neurologic and/or intellectual defects, a serum bilirubin determination is done routinely at approximately 48 hours of age on each Collaborative Study infant. Determinations are also done at other times as indicated by maternal history, clinical findings in the baby, such as jaundice, and if the routine test reveals a level greater than 10 mg.%. Thus some infants may have only the one routine test, while others may have as many as a dozen tests over a time span of several days. Approximately 10 per cent of 2,000 babies surveyed in the Johns Hopkins sample had hyperbilirubinemia, as indicated by one or more serum bilirubin determinations in excess of 10 mg.%. For purposes of data analysis the highest bilirubin value for each child is usually considered.

Some of the preliminary findings from the Collaborative Project with respect to serum bilirubin were presented by Boggs (1963). Table 6 shows the distribution of serum bilirubin values as a function of birth weight. This table shows that as the level of serum bilirubin rises an increasing percentage of babies are premature by weight.

Table 7 shows the developmental status of the child at eight months as a function of the highest serum bilirubin determination during the neonatal period. The developmental level was obtained by administering the Bayley Scale of Infant Development (Bayley, 1933). The children were rated normal, suspect, or abnormal. When the maximum serum bilirubin determination was below 11 mg.%, 85.8 per cent of the children were rated normal, as compared with only 66.4 per cent when the serum bilirubin was found to be 20 mg.% or above.

TABLE 6: Birth Weight as a Function of Highest Neonatal Serum Bilirubin Value

Birth Weight (gms.)	Highest Bilirubin Value (mg. %)										
	Under 11		11–15		16–17		18–19		20 & over		Totals	
	No.	%	No.	%	No.	%	No.	%	No.	%	No.	%
2,500 & under	1,016	7.4	229	17.3	48	22.4	39	29.3	48	24.7	1,380	8.8
2,501 & over	12,791	92.6	1,092	82.7	166	77.6	94	70.7	146	75.3	14,289	91.2
Total	13,807	100.0	1,321	100.0	214	100.0	133	100.0	194	100.0	15,669	100.0

SOURCE: Preliminary data, the Collaborative Perinatal Project, compiled by Boggs (1963).

TABLE 7: Developmental Status at Eight Months as a Function of Highest Neonatal Serum Bilirubin Value

Eight-Month Diagnosis	Highest Bilirubin Value (mg. %)										
	Under 11		11–15		16–17		18–19		20 & over		Totals	
	No.	%	No.	%	No.	%	No.	%	No.	%	No.	%
Abnormal	220	2.6	57	6.8	10	6.7	8	9.3	17	12.1	312	3.2
Suspect	1,002	11.6	126	15.0	33	22.1	19	22.1	30	21.4	1,210	12.3
Normal	7,403	85.8	655	78.2	106	71.2	59	68.6	93	66.5	8,316	84.5
Total	8,625	100.0	838	100.0	149	100.0	86	100.0	140	100.0	9,838	100.0

SOURCE: Preliminary data, the Collaborative Perinatal Project, compiled by Boggs (1963).

Table 8 shows the over-all neurologic status at one year of age for the surviving children in the project related to highest neonatal bilirubin value. The percentage of children rated abnormal whose maximum bilirubin determinations were below 11 mg.% was 1.7 as compared with 7.9 per cent of the children rated abnormal in the group whose maximum bilirubin level was 20 mg.% or above. There was a progressive increase in the rate of abnormality found with increasing bilirubin levels from 11 to 20 mg.%.

Figure 3 shows the frequency of abnormal neurologic status at one year of age in relation to birth weight as well as maximum serum bilirubin level. For a given bilirubin level, the smaller premature infants appear to have a higher frequency of neurologic abnormalities than the larger babies. At the 20 mg.% level, birth weight seems to produce little difference, but the numbers are very small, thus precluding the possibility of reliable comparisons.

Premature birth, particularly where the birth weight has been 1,500 gms. or less, has a well-recognized association with later handicapping mental and/or physical conditions. The underlying factors responsible for the relatively high incidence of defect in premature infants is not clear but in all probability there are multiple causes. It is well known that the small premature infant is more prone to cerebral hemorrhage, hypoxia, and the metabolic imbalance attendant upon hypoxia, hyperbilirubinemia, and immature renal function. Furthermore, premature delivery occurs with much greater frequency in the socially and economically underprivileged, where adequate prenatal and infant care may be lacking. Equally lacking in this group are

TABLE 8: Neurologic Status at One Year as a Function of Highest Neonatal Serum Bilirubin Value

Neuro. Findings at One Yr.	Highest Bilirubin Value (mg. %)											
	Under 11		11–15		16–17		18–19		20 & over		Totals	
	No.	%	No.	%	No.	%	No.	%	No.	%	No.	%
Abnormal	162	1.7	23	2.6	6	3.8	6	6.4	11	7.9	208	1.9
Suspect	618	6.5	83	9.3	17	10.9	10	10.6	15	10.8	743	6.9
Normal	8,684	91.8	787	88.1	133	85.3	78	83.0	113	81.3	9,795	91.2
Total	9,464	100.0	893	100.0	156	100.0	94	100.0	139	100.0	10,746	100.0

SOURCE: Preliminary data, the Collaborative Perinatal Project, compiled by Boggs (1963).

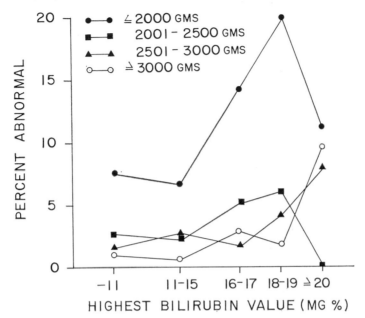

FIG. 3: Per cent distribution of neurologic abnormalities at one year of age by birth weight and highest neonatal serum bilirubin level. Preliminary data from the Collaborative Perinatal Project compiled by Boggs (1963).

opportunities for intellectual development. As a consequence it is difficult to pinpoint the relation between prematurity and retarded mental development, uncontaminated by other factors.

Some of the results of the long term study of Harper, Fischer, and Rider (1959) involving approximately 1,000 premature infants and a like number of normal controls born in 1952 are shown in Figure 4. Intelligence tests administered to the children at ages three and five years revealed that among those in the group who weighed 1,500 gms. or less at birth there was a higher incidence of defective and dull children, and fewer above average children, than in the group of larger premature infants or in the group of controls who weighed 2,501 gms. or above at birth. The larger premature infants were intermediate in performance. The Negro children in all weight groups performed significantly less well than the white children in the comparable weight group; the number of above average Negro children was small and there were none in the smallest weight category. Drillien (1961) showed that while the performance of premature infants as a whole

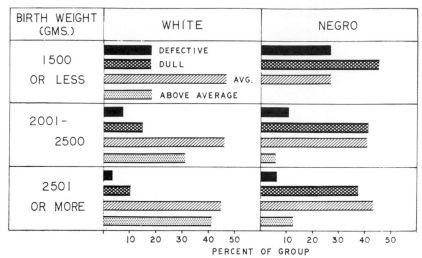

Fig. 4: Intelligence rating at three to five years by race and birth weight. Baltimore premature children. From Harper, Fischer, and Rider (1959) as arranged by Drillien (1961) and modified.

was poorer than that of full term controls, socio-economic and cultural factors as determined by "grade of mother" also played a role; the premature children at the lower social levels performed more poorly than those in the more privileged groups. This finding may be responsible for the observed Negro-white difference.

The results from Douglas' (1960) follow-up study on some 600 white children in England, shown in Figure 5, are similar to those of Harper. Two additional pieces of information presented by Douglas are of interest: first, that the behavior ratings by the teachers indicated that the children in the premature group presented more difficulties in school and generated more complaints than those in the mature group; and, second, that less than half of the premature children, as compared with the controls, passed the qualifying examination for admission to secondary school.

Table 9 shows mean IQ's of the children in the Hopkins Collaborative Study at age four, divided according to birth weight. It suggests, as did Harper's data, a positive correlation between birth weight and IQ at age four.

FOLLOW-UP STUDIES

We turn now to a consideration of the results of the psychologic examination of children in the Hopkins Collaborative

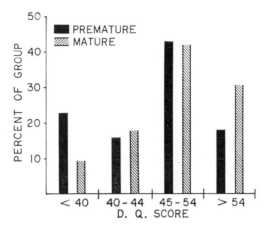

FIG. 5: Developmental quotients (DQ) of 600 eleven-year-old children as a function of prematurity. Modified from Douglas (1960). A developmental quotient score of 54 approximates an IQ score of 110.

TABLE 9: Mean IQ (Binet) at Four Years, by Race and Birth Weight

Birth Weight	Negro		White	
	No.	Mean IQ	No.	Mean IQ
2,500 gms. & under	14	88.6	0	—
2,501-3,000 gms.	58	92.6	13	92.7
3,001 gms. & over	109	94.4	33	99.7

NOTE: Excluded from the above calculations are: one Negro female who could not be adequately tested because of aberrant behavior, one white male who could not be adequately tested because of severe mental and motor handicaps (estimated IQ 50), and one white female of unknown birth weight (transferred from the Boston Study, IQ 121).

SOURCE: Preliminary data, the Johns Hopkins Collaborative Project.

Project, carried out close to the fourth birthday. An attempt was made to relate the psychologist's composite score of each four-year-old child to significant perinatal events. These data are presented in Tables 10 and 11. The composite score was based on the Stanford-Binet IQ score, Graham block sort score (Graham *et al.,* 1962) as a measure of concept information, evaluation of fine and gross motor skills, and a behavioral profile. For purposes of this analysis, children

TABLE 10: Psychologic Status of 179 Negro Children at Age Four Years

Category	Total No.	Sex		No. Premature	Adverse Perinatal Factors and Comments
		M	F		
Group I					
Psychologically suspect Neurologically normal	49	31	18	3	15 (4 with fetal distress)
Group II					
Psychologically suspect Neurologically suspect or abnormal	32	21	11	9	20 (in 9 cases, the neurologic deficit was probably acquired postnatally)
Total psychologically suspect	81	52	29	12	35
Group III					
Psychologically normal Neurologically normal	91	36	55	0	43 (8 with fetal distress)
Group IV					
Psychologically normal Neurologically suspect	7	4	3	2	4 (2 with fetal distress
Total psychologically normal	98	40	58	2	47

SOURCE: Preliminary data, the Johns Hopkins Collaborative Project.

scoring below 85 on the Binet, or below 23 on the Graham blocks, were considered psychologically suspect, as were children rated abnormal on the motor tests.

The heading "adverse perinatal factors" includes a number of obstetric and fetal factors believed to indicate risk. These include the following: chronic hypertension, toxemia of pregnancy, abruptio placentae, major hemorrhage prior to the birth of the infant, prolonged labor (over 30 hours), precipitous labor (under 2 hours), difficult delivery (midforceps or breech), and evidence of fetal distress during labor. An Apgar score of 4 or less and hyperbilirubinemia (15 mg.% or more) were also included among the adverse perinatal factors. Premature delivery per se was not included. In actual fact there were no babies weighing less than 2,200 gms. who were not at risk from one or more of the conditions listed above.

Table 10 shows a breakdown of the psychologic status of 179 Negro children at age four years in relation to sex, the presence of adverse

perinatal factors, and the recognition of abnormal or suspect neurologic findings at any time between the fourth-month examination
and four years of age. Table 11 shows the same data for the white
children, but because of small numbers, they were divided into two
psychologic categories only, (1) normal and (2) suspect and abnormal regardless of neurologic status. It will be noted that as
compared with the experience of the white children, there is a high
frequency of adverse perinatal factors in all Negro groups. In the

TABLE 11: Psychologic Status of 48 White Children at Age Four Years

Psychologic Category	No.		Adverse Perinatal Factors and Comments
Normal	28	3	
Suspect or Abnormal	20	14	(8 children were neurologically suspect or abnormal; 3 children in the group had no perinatal and no neurologic abnormalities)

SOURCE: Preliminary data, the Johns Hopkins Collaborative Project.

white children there seems to be a clear relationship between perinatal
events and suspect psychologic and neurologic status at age four years.
Perhaps this relationship is more clearly seen in the white group
because it is less clouded by adverse environmental circumstances. In
the Negro group, on the other hand, outcome at age four may in
some cases be the consequence of adverse perinatal events and in others
the result of environmental stresses, which are more frequent than
among the white children. Figure 6 and Table 12 provide data on the
actual IQ's of the Negro and white children in the Hopkins Collaborative Project. The Negro children do somewhat less well than the white
children. The females do better than the males in both groups.
This latter difference may reflect differential rates of maturation and/
or the fact that the Binet depends heavily on verbal ability in which
girls excel boys at that age. In order to evaluate the meaning of the
Negro-white differences, especially as to the role of postnatal environmental stress, it is necessary to equate the two groups on perinatal
complications.

If the subjects are divided into two groups, those with adverse
perinatal factors presumed to be stressful and those without adverse
perinatal factors, the IQ distribution changes, as shown in Table 13.
It may be noted from the data that the Negro group without perinatal
complications contains 4 children with clear postnatal trauma and 5

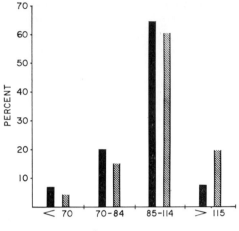

FIG. 6: Distribution of IQ (Binet) scores of 182 Negro and 48 white four-year-old children. The Johns Hopkins Collaborative Project (preliminary data). The scores of Negro children are represented by solid bars, those of white children by cross-hatched bars.

TABLE 12: Mean IQ (Binet) at Four Years by Race and Sex

Sex	Negro		White	
	No.	Mean IQ	No.	Mean IQ
Male	91	90.3	23 [a]	93.6
Female	90 [b]	96.6	24	100.3
Total tested	181	93.5	47	97.0

[a] White male excluded from calculations because severe mental and motor handicaps precluded adequate test; IQ estimated at 50.
[b] Negro female excluded from calculations because aberrant behavior precluded adequate test.

SOURCE: Preliminary data, the Johns Hopkins Collaborative Project.

others with probable postnatal trauma. If these 9 children are removed from the group, the mean IQ of the remaining children increases from 95.9 to 98.0. Examining the data as a whole allows for the conclusion that perinatal complications are definitely associated with a significant decrease in the IQ. The Negro-white differ-

TABLE 13: Distribution of Binet IQ Scores in Relation to Presumably Stressful Perinatal Factors

| | Adverse Perinatal Factors | | | |
| | Presumed present | | Presumed absent | |
	Mean IQ	No.	Mean IQ	No.
Negro	89.8	82	95.9	97 [a]
White	85.4	17	103.0	31

[a] Included in this group are four children with IQ's of 52, 67, 72, and 76, respectively, who have a clear history of postnatal insult. There are five other children with IQ scores ranging from 70–90 with probable postnatal insult. Without these nine children the mean IQ for this group becomes 98.0.

ences observed when the groups were compared without regard to birth factors now become neither consistent nor substantial. In the group with complications, there is a 4.4 difference in favor of the Negro children, while in the group without pre- or postnatal trauma there is a 5.0 difference in favor of the white children. It appears, therefore, that the greater incidence of perinatal complications in the Negro group accounts almost completely for the observed IQ differences reported earlier. This finding does not mean that socio-cultural variables play no role in the development of intelligence, but rather that among the children studied there were no profound socio-cultural differences.

SUMMARY

Some of the biologic factors that may influence intelligence have been reviewed with special reference to certain perinatal events. It would appear clear that perinatal factors do play a role in the causation of neurologic and intellectual deficits. It is reasonable to believe that there is a spectrum of deficit related to the severity of the injury sustained. However, it seems equally clear that perinatal factors represent only one segment in the succession of environmental circumstances to which the fetus and the child are exposed. The final result, be it a highly intelligent contributing member of society, or a mental defective, is the product of complex interaction between the genetic endowment and the total environment.

REFERENCES

APGAR, VIRGINIA. Evaluation of the newborn infant—second report. *J.A.M.A.*, 1958, **168**, 1985–1988.

BATTAGLIA, F., FRAZIER, T., & HELLEGERS, A. Obstetric and pediatric complications of juvenile pregnancy. *Pediat.*, 1963, **32**, 902–910.

BAYLEY, N. Mental growth during the first three years: a developmental study of sixty-one children by repeated tests. *Genet. Psychol. Monogr.*, 1933, **14**, 1–92 (as modified in 1958 for use in the Collaborative Perinatal Project, Perinatal Research Branch, National Institute of Neurological Diseases and Blindness, Bethesda, Maryland).

BENDA, C. E. *Developmental disorders of mentation and the cerebral palsies.* New York: Grune and Stratton, 1952.

BERG, J. M., & KERMAN, B. H. The mentally defective twin. *Brit. Med. J.*, 1959, **1**, 1911–1917.

BOGGS, T. R. Preliminary data with respect to the relationship of highest serum bilirubin to certain other findings in the Collaborative Project. Presented at the spring scientific meeting of the Collaborative Perinatal Project, National Institute of Neurological Diseases and Blindness, Washington, 1963.

COURVILLE, C. B. Ultimate residual lesions of antenatal and neonatal asphyxia. *A.M.A. Am. J. Dis. Child.*, 1952, **84**, 64–78.

———. Antenatal and paranatal circulatory disorders as a cause of cerebral damage early in life. *J. Neuropath.*, 1959, **18**, 115–140.

DOUGLAS, J. W. B. Premature children at primary schools. *Brit. Med. J.*, 1960, **1**, 1008–1013.

DRILLIEN, C. M. Growth and development in a group of children of very low birthweight. *Arch. Disease in Childhood*, 1958, **33**, 10–18.

———. A longitudinal study of the growth and development of prematurely and maturely born children. Part VII. Mental development. *Arch. Disease in Childhood*, 1961, **36**, 233–240.

EASTMAN, N. J., KOHL, S. G., MAISEL, J. E., & KAVALER, F. The obstetrical background of 753 cases of cerebral palsy. *Obst. and Gyn. Survey*, 1962, **17**, 459–500.

GRAHAM, F. K., ERNHART, C. B., THURSTON, D., & CRAFT, M. Development three years after perinatal anoxia and other potentially damaging newborn experiences. *Psychol. Monogr.*, 1962, **76**, No. 3 (Whole No. 522).

GREENBERG, M., PELLITTERI, O., & BARTON, J. Frequency of defects in infants whose mothers had rubella during pregnancy. *J.A.M.A.*, 1957, **165**, 675–678.

GREGG, M. M. Rubella during pregnancy of mother with its sequelae of congenital defects in child. *M. J. Australia*, 1945, **1**, 313–315.

HARPER, P. A. *Preventive pediatrics.* New York: Appleton-Century-Crofts, 1962.

HARPER, P. A., FISCHER, L. K., & RIDER, R. V. Neurologic and intellectual status of prematures at three to five years of age. *J. Pediat.*, 1959, **55**, 679–690.

HENDERSON, M., ENTWISLE, G., & TAYBACK, M. Prevalence of significant asymptomatic bacteriuria and its association with prematurity. Presented before Epidemiology Section, Annual Meeting Am. Pub. Health Assoc., Detroit, 1961.

HUNT, J. McV. *Intelligence and experience.* New York: Ronald Press, 1961.

KASS, E. M. Bacteriuria and the prevention of prematurity and perinatal death. In *Physiology of prematurity.* Transactions of the Fifth Conf., Josiah Macy Jr. Foundation, 1961.

KENNEDY, C., DRAGE, J. S., & SCHWARTZ, B. K. Preliminary data with respect to the relationships between Apgar score at one and five minutes and fetal outcome: presented at the spring scientific meeting of the Collaborative Perinatal Project, National Institute of Neurological Diseases and Blindness, Washington, 1963.

KLATSKIN, E. H. Relationship of deficits in intelligence test performance of preschool children to perinatal experience. *J. Consult. Psychol.,* 1964, **28**, 228–233.

KNOBLOCH, H., & PASAMANICK, B. Syndrome of minimal brain damage in infancy. *J.A.M.A.,* 1959, **170**, 1384–1387.

LILIENFELD, A. M., & PARKHURST, E. A study of the association of the factors of pregnancy and parturition with the development of cerebral palsy. *Am. J. Hyg.,* 1951, **53**, 262–282.

LILIENFELD, A. M., PASAMANICK, B., & ROGERS, M. Relationship between pregnancy experience and the development of certain neuropsychiatric disorders in childhood. *Am. J. Publ. Health,* 1955, **45**, 637–643.

LITTLE, W. J. On the influence of abnormal parturition, difficult labour, premature birth, and asphyxia neonatorum, on the mental and physical condition of the child, especially in relation to deformities. *Trans. of the London Obst. Soc.,* 1862, **3**, 293.

MEDEARIS, D. N. Observations concerning human cytomegalovirus infection and disease. *Bull. Johns Hopkins Hospital,* 1964, **3**, 181–211.

MICHAELS, R. H., & MELLIN, G. W. Prospective experience with maternal rubella and the associated congenital malformation. *Pediatrics,* 1960, **26**, 200–209.

PAINE, R. S. Minimal chronic brain syndrome in children. *Develop. Med. Child Neurol.,* 1962, **4**, 21–27.

PARKMAN, P. D., BUESCHER, E. L., & ARTENSTEIN, M. S. Recovery of rubella virus from army recruits. *Proc. Soc. Exp. Biol. Med.,* 1962, **111**, 225–230.

PENROSE, L. S. *The biology of mental defect* (3d ed.). London: Sidgwick & Jackson, 1963.

PRECHTL, H. F. R., & STEMMER, J. The choreiform syndrome in children. *Develop. Med. Child Neurol.,* 1962, **4**, 119–127.

RIDER, R. V., TAYBACK, M., & KNOBLOCH, H. Association between premature birth and socio-economic status. *Am. J. Publ. Health,* 1955, **45**, 1022–1028.

ROWE, W. P. Adenovirus and salivary gland virus infections in children. In H. M. Rose (Ed.), *Viral infections of infancy and childhood.* Symposium of The Section on Microbiology, New York Acad. Med. No. 10. New York: Paul B. Hoeber, 1960.

SEVER, J. L., SCHIFF, G. M., & HUEBNER, R. J. The prevalence of rubella antibody among pregnant women and other human and animal populations. Preliminary data presented at the spring meeting of the Collaborative Perinatal Project, National Institute of Neurological Diseases and Blindness, Washington, 1963.

STEWART, A. A note on the obstetric effect of work during pregnancy. *Brit. J. Prev. Soc. Med.,* 1955, **9**, 159–161.

WELLER, T. H., & NEVA, F. A. Propagation in tissue culture of cytopathic agents from patients with rubella-like illness. *Proc. Soc. Exp. Biol. Med.,* 1962, **111**, 215–225.

WINDLE, W. F., BECKER, R. F., & WEIL, A. Alterations in brain structure after asphyxiation at birth: an experimental study in the guinea pig. *J. Neuropath. and Exper. Neurol.,* 1944, **3**, 224–238.

4

EFFECTS OF EARLY DEPRIVATION OF PHOTIC STIMULATION

Austin Riesen

The relationship between seeing and mental development, I think, is fairly obvious. Many performances that are not directly under the control of vision nevertheless depend upon prior visual experience. In a very excellent review of capabilities of the blind, Dr. Axelrod in 1959 reported results of several tests on which, with vision excluded, performance reflects earlier interaction with a visual environment. Tests of abstraction and tests of complex tactually perceived patterns are more difficult for persons who have never seen. The transfer of learning sets between tactile and auditory modalities is affected by whether or not there has been adequate prior visual experience. In other words, there are cross-modality percepts which develop gradually through early experience and which are a permanent part of the mental capacity of the organism. A graduate student who has just finished his research at Chicago, Paul D. Wilson, has some interesting data on infant rhesus monkeys. I will refer to these later. By way of introduction here I simply mention the fact that in a simple motor task of thumb-finger opposition, the holding back of pattern vision during the early days of life retards the monkey's initial use of this type of interaction with his environment. With normal monkeys, as demonstrated by an early study done by Hines (1942), forty-two

Austin Riesen, Ph.D., is professor of psychology, University of California at Riverside.

days is the age at which the rhesus monkey first exhibits thumb-finger opposition. This is tested without visual control, with an object presented to touch. With or without visual control, monkeys that have seen only diffused light during the first twenty days of life do not start showing thumb-finger opposition until nine days later than do the normal animals.

We know that mental development and behavioral development are intimately related. We are often uncertain as to which precedes and which follows, because neither proceeds far without the other. The problem needs to be restated in somewhat more concrete terms, which will be done in the form of four hypotheses. We may begin with one hypothesis, which is highly favored, and this is that organic growth yields behavioral growth. We know from some of the recent work of Levi-Montalcini (1964) in St. Louis that there are protein nerve growth factors that are critical in embryonic development. These can selectively affect different parts of the nervous system. When the development has reached a certain stage, even in the embryo, certain behavioral responses are possible. Now our second hypothesis, sometimes opposed to the first as an exclusive alternative, which I think is quite unnecessary, is that behaviors are dependent upon stimulation for development. Our third hypothesis is that changes in neural structure result under conditions that produce behavioral development or behavioral arrest. And here I might add a corollary to the effect that optimum stimulation maximizes structural and functional growth in the visual system. I choose the visual system in this instance because of some practical experimental considerations which will become clear as we examine the data. The fourth hypothesis, about which many people are skeptical, is that low functional levels induce irreversible cell atrophy, resulting in permanent behavioral arrest.

Let us examine these hypotheses in turn. I would like to start first with some of the better evidence that innate behavioral organization evolves as a function of growth, almost without consideration of any detailed correlations between growth and function. Assuming proper nutrition and other background environmental factors, we can find at birth in many vertebrate organisms ocular-motor behavior that is ready to function. The opto-kinetic response is familiar and is a useful indicator of this function. The head as well as the eyes will turn as a consequence of motion of the total visual field. This is demonstrated in newborn primates within a few hours of birth (McGinnis, 1930), and in those that have had only diffused light from birth at somewhat older ages. The visual pursuit of a light may be rather difficult to demonstrate in a newborn human being or primate, but within a few days it appears. If we keep that organism in diffused light, so that he has no target to fixate, then, as we remove the diffused light conditions and introduce for the first time a light which may move in the visual environment, there is the fixation and jerky pursuit movement, which includes eye muscle participation. This behavior is organized on the basis of the innate development of the nervous system. Also similarly organized are the pupillary responses to changes in light intensity and other reflexes. We have, then, at least this body of evidence supporting hypothesis one in the case of ocular-motor behavior and of head-orienting movements.

There are other dimensions of neural function that show relationships with different stimuli, and again we can demonstrate some of these in the absence of the opportunity of the organism to develop them by experience. One of these is in the organization of response to difference in the wave length of visual stimulation. Dr. Leo Ganz about four years ago raised some monkeys in diffused light, some in total darkness, and some under normal environmental conditions. In all cases he then presented to these animals only one wave length in the visual spectrum and trained them to press a lever during the presentation of this light (Ganz and Riesen, 1962). The animals learned not to press when that particular visual stimulus was not present, i.e., in darkness. He then tested for generalization of the response to other hues. The data obtained are presented in Figure 1. These data summarize the responses to colors that were removed in steps of 30 millimicrons each from the hue used in training. The monkeys received initial stimulation only at one end of the visual spectrum, or at one value two steps from the extreme. They were otherwise either dark-reared or diffused-light-reared. The data in the light-deprived animals were actually so similar that we combined the dark-reared and the diffused-light-reared, and compared them here with the experienced or normal animals. A gradient of response rates reflects the degree to which each color is removed in the visual spectrum from the others. Two animals are represented in each curve. The different wave lengths were presented in random sequence during testing. There was never any reinforcement for responding to any of the stimuli except the one used in training. We have here, clearly, evidence of an organization of the visual system somewhere between the receptor cone system and the central brain structure. Here again is support for hypothesis one.

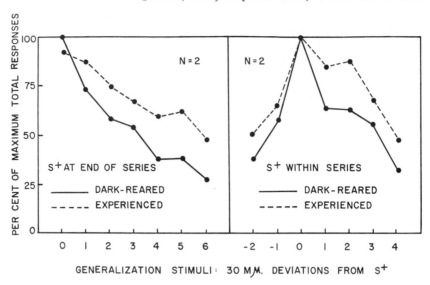

GENERALIZATION GRADIENTS TO HUE IN DARK-REARED AND

NORMALLY-REARED MONKEYS

Fig. 1: Results with eight monkeys on tests of stimulus generalization along the wave length continuum. Responding was reinforced only at the zero value on the abscissa. (From Riesen, 1961.)

Hypothesis two stated that there are certain kinds of visual behavior which come under control of the nervous system only after experience of selective types. Some of the work at Brandeis and MIT by Held and Hein indicates that under some conditions animals must react with motor responses to a visual environment if they are to organize their behavior properly, if they are to avoid obstacles, if they are to respond to a table edge with the typical visual placing response (Held and Hein, 1963).

We have some recent data, which have just been published in the new journal, *Psychonomic Science* (Riesen, Ramsey, and Wilson, 1964), indicating that visual acuity is not fully developed if the organism has seen only diffused light. In rhesus monkeys that were kept in diffused light from birth to twenty days, or from birth to sixty days, initial response in the opto-kinetic drum, and the initial thresholds for discriminating horizontal from vertical lines in a learned visual discrimination were considerably higher than in normal animals of the same age. However, as these animals were brought into patterned light the improvement began immediately. They showed, much to our surprise, progressive improvement closely parallel to that of normally developing rhesus monkeys starting from birth. A rhesus monkey's eye and nervous structures are better developed at birth than are the human infant's. The development of acuity in these animals is correspondingly more advanced. Figure 2 presents data on visual acuity of animals reared in diffused light as compared to four newborn animals.

The increased threshold represents only one effect of pattern deprivation in the visual environment of the infant rhesus monkey. These and other animals, reared in diffused light for twenty or sixty days, developed other kinds of visual behavior in the first two days of patterned experience on a schedule which was as good, or perhaps

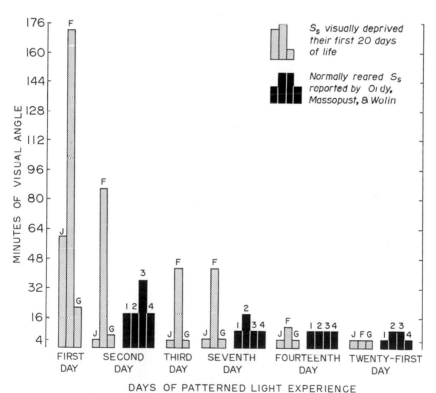

FIG. 2: The development of visual acuity of monkeys after deprivation of pattern vision from birth to twenty days. The ordinate indicates resolution thresholds. (From Riesen, Ramsey, and Wilson, 1964)

a little bit better; that is, they actually came along a little more rapidly than newborn rhesus monkeys (Wilson, 1964). As normal controls, we have a sample that represents primarily the study of Hines (1942), but also data from one monkey raised by Lashley and Watson (1913), and one raised by Foley (1934). In the case of initial visual pursuit of a moving object, normal animals show this behavior between the fourth and the twenty-eighth day. Wilson's animals in our Chicago laboratory showed this between the fourth and the twelfth day after exposure to a normal visual environment. The visual placing response in the newborn rhesus monkeys shows up between the sixth and twenty-first day, for normals, and between days five and sixteen for the diffused-light-reared animals. The days were counted from day twenty or day sixty, whichever represented the start of their patterned light experience. Starting at one age or the other proved to be unimportant.

The visual cliff test, quite famous from the studies at Cornell (Walk and Gibson, 1961), does not yet provide normative data starting immediately after birth, although Dr. Robert Fantz is in the process of obtaining such data. In the diffused-light-reared animals the earliest appearance of the visual cliff "depth" discrimination is two weeks after the beginning of patterned light experience. The range is fourteen to twenty-one days. Avoidance by eye closure to a threatened blow to the face begins occurring in Wilson's animals at approximately eighteen days after the diffused light condition is terminated. Where we find scattered data on animals tested from birth, this response first appears considerably later than eighteen days. We have one example in which behavior in diffused-light-reared animals occurs later, in terms of days, after exposure to a normal visual environment. Under Wilson's conditions it took twenty days of patterned light before monkeys discriminated between a triangle and a circle, whereas in Zimmermann's monkeys this appeared by the tenth day. In terms of trials, however, the actual training time was not different, since Wilson gave half as many trials as did Zimmermann (Wilson, 1964; Zimmerman, 1961).

All of these behaviors are examples of those which are not immediately present in animals reared under diffused light, nor are they present in the newborn animal. They show up in the monkey much earlier than in the human, indicating that first of all we must have sufficient maturation of the structure underlying this behavior. In addition we must have a minimum amount of pattern experience which extends from ten hours up to very many hours and days, depending on the particular response required.

This is one category of information indicating that hypothesis two is tenable: that there are behaviors in the visual perception of the environment which require experience and interaction with that environment. This statement applies with particular force to primates. Some studies of chimpanzees that we reared from birth to seven months in diffused light are in point here.

Visual stimuli were presented singly to the young animal in a training series begun on the day after it was brought into a normal visual environment, or at a comparable age in the control animal. The stimulus discs were painted with a series of stripes, alternating in color, each stripe 5 cm. wide. The large yellow and black disc with vertical stripes was 38 cm. in diameter. This was shown in front of the animal for five seconds at a distance of 40 cm., and then advanced quickly to the face. A mild shock to the lower chin was delivered until the animal turned its face aside. If he turned away during the five seconds of presentation, the shock was avoided. Following a stable response of avoidance, discs were shown in a random order. All other discs were followed by food, so the animal learned to approach them. If it approached, then the feeding bottle was presented at the mouth. Needless to say the shock was never severe enough to prevent the animal from returning to the food on a subsequent presentation.

Two daily sessions, six presentations at each, were given to each animal until a criterion of eighteen consecutive correct responses occurred. Depending upon the disc, correct response was based on one of the following cues: (1) direction of stripe, (2) color, (3) size, or (4) outline form.

Table 1 shows, first, that there is some difference between the diffused-light-reared animals, the "experimental" group, and the controls in the trial of the initial anticipatory disturbance, indicating recognition of the shock plaque. The first evidence of learning was after a mean of 13.5 trials for the experimental group, and only 3.7 for controls. Active avoidance was considerably later in two of the experimentals. Animal No. 119 was a control that was in patterned light only ninety minutes per day; the remaining twenty-two and one-half hours he was in total darkness. The other two controls were animals with normal visual experience. There is no overlap between the two groups. We gained confidence in these data primarily because other supporting evidence with monkeys and with cats points to similar conclusions, as will be seen in what comes later.

Once a given animal had learned to avoid the shock disc, the other four discs were introduced, each time followed by the feeding bottle ten seconds later. Table 1 shows that there was a large difference between the two groups in the total number of trials required before the discriminative behavior was sufficiently stable for the criterion to be met.

It is important to know whether the various stimuli were equally difficult for the experimental animals, those having had diffused light for seven months. Table 2 shows that they were not equally difficult

TABLE 1: Learned Avoidance Response to Large Black and Yellow Disc, Followed by Discriminations Based on Color, Size, Horizontal-Vertical, and Outline Form

Animal Number	Conditioned Emotional Response and Conditioned Avoidance		Discrimination Learning
	Trial to First Anticipatory Disturbance	Trial to First Avoidance Effort	Trials to Criterion
Experimentals			
125	9	20	534
142	14	26	1056
168	22	22	678
145	9	9	978
Average	13.5	19.2	811
Controls			
119	7	7	240
101	3	5	216
107	1	1	230
Average	3.7	4.3	229

TABLE 2: Total Errors to Criterion Learning (Three Feedings without Error)

Animal Number	Experimentals				Controls			
	125	142	168	Totals	119	101	107	Totals
Horizontal	5	24	12	41	6	16	19	41
Red	16	16	7	39	6	17	17	40
Small	44	17	7	68	0	13	9	22
Square	93	89	30	212	5	20	18	43
Shock-disc	9	117	47	173	35	9	15	59
Totals	167	263	103	533	52	75	78	205

by any means. The horizontal-vertical discrimination shows the same number of errors for the three controls as for the three experimentals. (In this case we omitted one animal, No. 145, which had rather marked exophoria and spontaneous nystagmus. The others had eliminated these symptoms without difficulty. No. 145 also had exposure to a special flicker stimulating condition.) The red vs. yellow, or color discrimination, was not different for the two groups. The size gave some difficulty, especially to No. 125. The large increase in errors for the experimentals was due primarily to the difficulty of form discrimination: square vs. circle. This difference accounts for the confusion between the shock disc and the food rewarded plaques. For the control animals, none of the stimuli was markedly different in difficulty from the others.

Total errors were 205 vs. 533, or on the average per animal, 68 for the control group, 178 for the experimental. There was no overlap in individual totals between the groups. A major source of difference lies in the "false" approaches to the shock disc.

The experimental animals above were chimpanzees reared in diffused light from birth to seven months. In these particular animals light diffusion was all carried out through a dome over the animal's face during two 45-minute sessions per day. In our cat studies we have some comparable effects after a shorter period of neonatal deprivation. Figure 3 shows the stimuli we used. The form discrimination was a triangle vs. circle problem. Moving vs. non-moving discriminations were given in two versions: rotating X vs. stationary X, and "bouncing" vs. stationary black circles. When presented to the animal, the X was always stationary on one of two windows in the Yerkes box, and the other one was rotating at 10 revolutions per minute. The animal was rewarded for consistent response to the moving or the non-moving.

We found this to be difficult even for normal cats (Riesen and Aarons, 1959) although they all learned it. In another series of experiments, we therefore tried the type of movement in which the black circle remained stationary in one window and oscillated up and down for a distance of 14 cm. in a 21.5-cm. square, this oscillation being one cycle per second. This moving stimulus is very obvious to the human being. The normally reared cat eventually learns this also, but is not very quick about it.

In a series of experiments, some of which are here reported for the first time, four rearing conditions were used. All kittens were reared from birth in the laboratory, left with their mothers until weaning at

FORM DISCRIMINATION

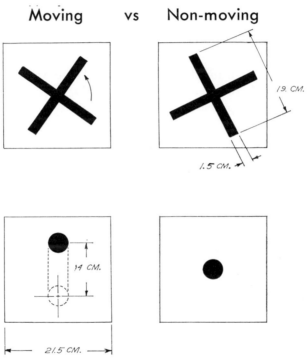

FIG. 3: Stimuli presented to diffused-light-reared cats. The form and movement discriminations required that cats learn to approach consistently (to a criterion of 90 per cent or better) one stimulus of a pair.

eight weeks, and then kept two to a cage. The first, or "normal," group lived in the well-lighted laboratory. The others lived in a dark-room. Beginning at six weeks they were brought into either a lighted laboratory for one hour of unrestricted play in a play area (group two) or brought into a similar patterned environment but held in a holder (group three), so that movement of their legs was independent of any consequence to the visual environment. They were free to rotate their heads and to fixate with their eyes their complex visual environment. Finally, animals of the fourth group were raised with one hour daily of diffused light, comparable to the chimpanzees behind the dome.

The largest difference in our results on movement discrimination (Riesen and Aarons, 1959) is between the unrestricted kittens and the form-deprived (diffused-light-reared) and restricted motor animals: the latter two groups failed to learn even with 3,600 or 4,000 trials, while the unrestricted kittens learned in less than half this number of trials. With two restricted and two form-deprived cats Aarons brought the surroundings closer to the edge of the rotating X, hoping to facilitate movement perception, but that did not seem to help, strangely enough. Immediately after this failure to learn movement discrimination, the cats readily learned to respond in the apparatus to intensity differences in fewer than 10 per cent as many trials.

We have more recently replicated and extended the study of effects of the four rearing conditions. In the new series all kittens learned intensity discriminations first. The groups showed no significant differences. The bar graph (Figure 4) shows this result, in which the left bar for each of four groups represents the average trials to a criterion of thirty-six correct responses out of forty on an initial intensity habit and its reversal.

The second problem given to each group was the discrimination of horizontal vs. vertical bands. An initial habit and its reversal were learned. Half of the animals in each group were trained to the horizontal first, and the others to the vertical first, until they performed at the 90 per cent criterion. Then a reversal of the habit completed the work on this form of discrimination. Again the differences were not significant, as with the chimpanzees.

The third visual discrimination problem was a stationary vs. moving dot, and in the fourth a difficult form discrimination, requiring the discrimination between X and N, was presented. The restricted motor and form-deprived animals performed very poorly on the last two problems. Ordering individuals on the trials that were required to learn initial habits (i.e., disregarding reversals entirely), the significance of each difference was examined by application of the Mann-Whitney U-test. In the stationary-moving and the X-N form discriminations, seven intergroup differences reached significance at the .05 level or beyond. All seven of these were among the eight possible

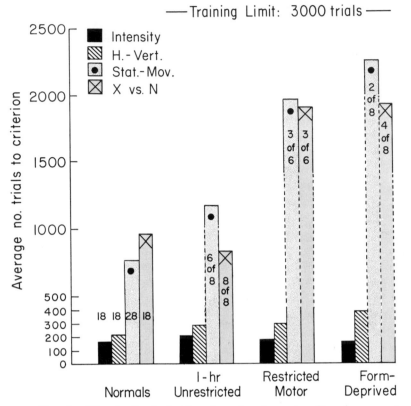

FIG. 4: Visual discrimination learning by cats after four rearing conditions.

comparisons between the members of the first two groups and those of the restricted and form-deprived groups.

We have evidence, then, that visual intensity discriminations are readily learned by animals, even after diffused light rearing. We have some additional data indicating that total darkness until sixteen weeks of age is not deleterious for the discrimination of intensity, where the brightnesses are sufficiently different (Aarons, Halasz, and Riesen, 1963). If the brightness difference is near the threshold, then early visual experience may be crucial. Restriction to diffused light or deprivation of patterned vision produces severe handicaps in some tasks and none in others.

The next data indicate that some of these effects can be restricted to one eye (Riesen and Mellinger, 1956). Figure 5 shows a comparison

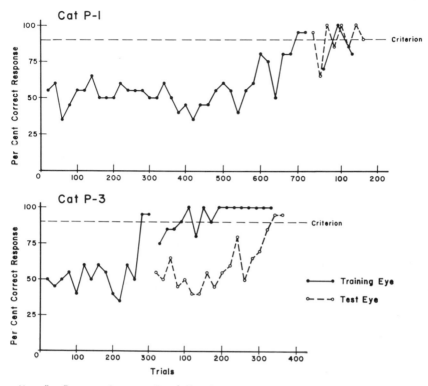

Fɪɢ. 5: Interocular transfer following criterion learning with one "train-ing eye" open. (From Riesen and Mellinger, 1956.)

between two representative kittens. Cat P-1 was an animal that had pattern experience alternately in the two eyes every day for two hours. In cat P-3 one eye was kept occluded with a diffuser so that it received diffused light; the other eye received pattern vision during two hours a day. In P-1 when one eye was used in training of a triangle vs. circle discrimination, the other eye showed the behavior at the same level on the initial twenty trials. Some fluctuation in transfer followed, which is characteristic following alternating monocular visual experi-ence. We obtained a range of transfer from about 60 per cent up to 90 per cent, where we used alternating stimulation as the prior experience. When we used binocular stimulation we got full transfer, 90 per cent or better. When we kept one eye in diffused light, the test eye, we found a split-brain type of syndrome. These data (cf. cat P-3 of Figure 5) look remarkably like those of Dr. Roger Sperry's split-brain animals (Sperry, 1961). The learning curve for the second eye traces almost a complete repetition of that for the first over the initial 300 trials. While the second eye was trained the first eye maintained its original performance. Some cats did better than this one, remaining consistently above the 90 per cent criterion. Chow and Nissen (1955) have done work with the chimpanzee under similar conditions and obtained comparable results.

Additional evidence on the role of stimulation in perceptual development comes from diffused light animals trained monocularly. They bump into objects when the unused eye is open and see and avoid them with the other eye, a behavior that reminds ophthalmologists strongly of the amblyope, or an individual with a "lazy eye," in an extreme form. These chimpanzees which we have been discussing recovered so that they saw well with either eye after anywhere from six weeks to a year. The actual progress was rather variable, and there were indications in the data, both from the chimpanzees and the cats, that rate of recovery depended a great deal on the animal's spontaneous activity level. Those that were highly active in their daily environment were the first ones to show full utilization of vision. We had a few cats that even after eighteen months were still bumping into objects. These were cats that were relatively passive, moving about in their living environment always with extreme caution. This kind of self-paced rate of learning was indicated by much of our data. It is not unlike the variation reported in patients after operation for early blindness.

We think that these facts represent differences in the fine structure of the nervous system. But how much can we tell about the fine structure? At what levels can we get either physiological or cytochemical or histological evidence?

Electrophysiological Measurements. When a small electrode is in contact with the cornea, and another is at a neutral point on the head or on the ear of a monkey or a cat, we get a recording that schematically looks like that of Figure 6. The first deflection is the a-wave, followed by what is called the b-wave. These reflect activity of receptors and transmitting bipolar cells, respectively, of the retina.

For the most part we have not found much change in the a-wave with dark rearing, although we think that eventually there is some change there. The b-wave is the one we measured and typically we took as the baseline the value just before the start of the a-wave and measured in microvolts the peak of upward deflection. If we used a

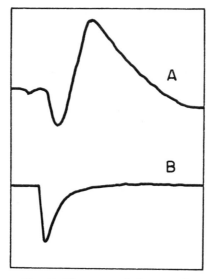

Fig. 6: The normal electroretino-
gram of the cat. "B" is the line
describing the time course of our
light flash. On "A" the downward
deflection is the a-wave, and the
upward   deflection   the   b-wave.
(From Baxter and Riesen, 1961)

weak light, the dark-reared animals did not show any progressive
changes in the b-wave with intervals of ten seconds (Baxter and
Riesen, 1961). However, the successive flashes at higher intensities produced a progressively diminishing b-wave as shown in Figure 7.

In normal cats all five intensities produce curves that are flat. In
the case of the monkey we have now used shorter times between
flashes in order to maximize the effect and also to show that this is
not an atypical b-wave shrinkage, even under normal conditions.
It is not a physiological freak, in other words.

Figure 8 shows that if the flashes are intense, and they are two
seconds apart, even the normal monkey shows some b-wave amplitude
shrinkage after the initial flash. These are averages for normal
rhesus monkeys, where the second flash produces a response that is
about 75 per cent of the first and then stays at about 70 per cent
indefinitely with continuing flashes at two-second intervals.

After five weeks without light, animals that have previously

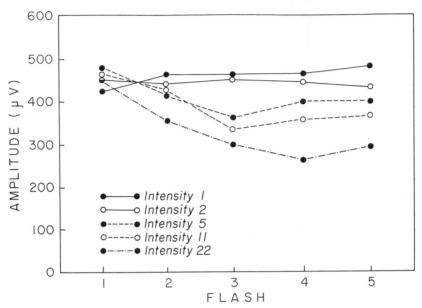

Fig. 7: Amplitudes of b-wave deflections in cats at twelve months of age after dark rearing. Successive flashes were ten seconds apart. (From Baxter and Riesen, 1961)

looked like the normals show a marked diminution of the second response, and with a third flash the b-wave amplitude is very small. It remains low for an indefinite period of time if we keep flashing every two seconds.

Figure 9 shows a series of responses from a young monkey, obtained by Robert Ramsey in our laboratory. The animal had been light-deprived, and the b-wave scarcely brings the record back to its base line. If there were no b-wave, this record would stay below base line due to the continuing a-wave, as recently shown by Brown and Watanabe (1962). It is just our arbitrary amplitude criterion which perhaps exaggerates the relative effect. Now this b-wave diminution is most easily explained, we think, in terms of some failure to recover in the transmission mechanism of the retina. Careful recent work indicates that it is probably a function of the transmission at the outer plexiform layer, the bipolar cells responding to the receptor cells, as it were. So perhaps the lack of stimulation results in the slowing down of bipolar cell recovery.

The first indication of chronic retinal change that we obtained

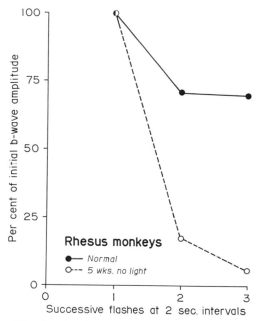

FIG. 8: Amplitude of b-wave in successive responses to intense light with normal and light-deprived monkeys.

from prolonged dark-reared animals was with the chimpanzees. Something was going seriously wrong with the retina, as revealed by our early observations of disc pallor which Dr. W. J. Knauer in Jacksonville, Florida, noticed in 1948 in our first chimpanzees. That is why we began using the diffused light condition in our later work. Those first animals had been in almost constant darkness for 16 months. Subsequently we had found this pallor showing up in chimpanzees in total darkness after a period of under a half year. Disc pallor resulting from exposure to total darkness up to a period of seven months disappears with subsequent normal stimulation. Somewhere before eighteen months the effect becomes irreversible and the disc never again looks completely normal. Histologically there are very obvious changes in these cells, in that the ganglion cells shrink in size and in the chimpanzees eventually many of them disappear. Brattgård (1952) reported confirming and beautifully quantified evidence of RNA losses in the ganglion cells of dark-reared rabbits.

Figures 10a and 10b show a chimpanzee retina from one of the diffused light animals. This animal had diffused light from birth to

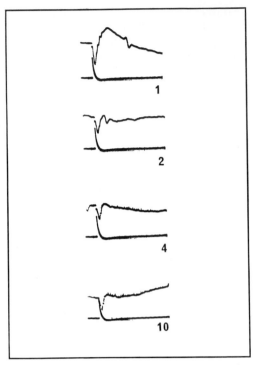

FIG. 9: Electro-retinogram responses to the first, second, fourth, and tenth flashes at two-second intervals in a light-deprived monkey. (From records by R. L. Ramsey)

seven months, ninety minutes a day, and after seven months was moved into a normal environment. The disc pallor, which was very slight at seven months, although Dr. Knauer thought there was a little bit there, disappeared in the succeeding months. This animal was two years and nine months old when it suddenly developed a rapid terminal illness, which was one of three cases in the colony over a period of fourteen years that were diagnosed as meningitis. While the retina looked healthy enough, we compared it with Polyak's slides on primates to verify our impressions of its essential normality. Since the rearing conditions were like those of our other animals we used this as our control (Chow, Riesen, and Newell, 1957). The ganglion cell layer here is, about like a human retina, from six to eight or nine cells deep. The bipolar cells and the receptor cells are also comparable.

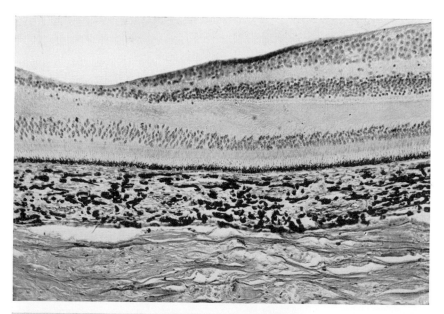

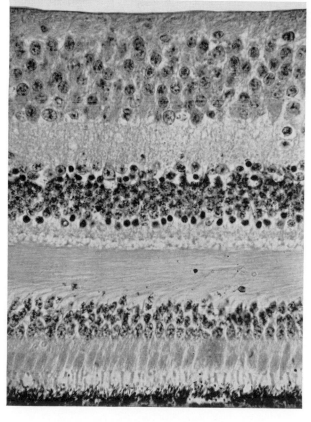

Fig. 10a: Fovea and temporal retina of Kora, diffused light and normal light given to age thirty-three months. X 160, hematoxylin and eosin. (Figures 10a–10d from K. L. Chow, A. H. Riesen, and F. W. Newell, *J. Comp. Neurol.*, **107**, 41–42 [Plates 1–8].)

b: Left parafovea of Kora under higher magnification.

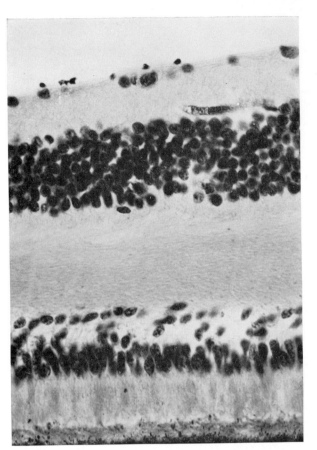

c: Left parafovea of dark-reared chimpanzee, showing atrophy of the ganglion cell layer.

d: Fovea of chimpanzee, Faik, deprived of visual stimulation from the age of eight months to twenty-four months. Note few remaining ganglion cells.

Figure 10c shows what happened to a dark-reared animal. Receptors and bipolars are not reduced in number, but 90 per cent of the ganglion cells are gone. This animal had no light stimulation from birth to thirty-three months, and then had normal stimulation for several years during which we followed his behavior. There was a little pupillary reflex left initially and that gradually faded. But it is difficult to say whether these remaining ganglion cells do anything functionally. Perhaps they are to some degree involved in efferent neural activity, as demonstrated by Granit and others for the visual system.

Figure 10d shows another animal, under lower power. The temporal retina from the center on out has a few ganglion cells. This animal still had a weak pupillary response to bright light, so it is apparent some of the cells were still working. There was no loss in cell population in receptors or bipolars. Obviously the fiber layer has shriveled away and the disc pallor is pretty well explained. This animal was in a normal environment up to eight months and in the dark room from eight to twenty-four months. We have not found this type of effect in the cat, in that the cells do not disappear even after dark rearing from birth to thirty-nine months. With this picture obviously we would expect a trans-neuronal effect in the lateral geniculate body of the animal, and its degeneration proved to be extensive. Excellent comparisons of stimulated and deafferented laminae of cat lateral geniculate nuclei have been carried out by Cook, Walker, and Barr (1951) and by Kupfer and Palmer (1964). Drs. Paul Coleman and Van der Loos have some cat eyes which we hope will demonstrate whether this kind of stimulus deprivation does anything at the cortical level. Preliminary findings indicate reductions in dendritic branchings. They are in general similar but less extensive than Jones and Thomas (1962) have reported in surgical deafferentation of olfactory cortical cells. Both approaches result in loss of, or reduced development of, branches removed from the primary trunks.

Table 3 shows another approach we have been taking in the investigation of effects of reduced stimulation. The RNA concentration of the ganglion cells of the dark-reared cat drops to about half of the normal. In this series, with an age range from four to thirty-nine months, there is no clear relationship to the age. Once the dark-reared cat has reached four months, apparently its RNA stays level at about 40 to 50 per cent of the normal. Three cats had normal light for one hour a day, and this resulted in intermediate levels of RNA. The reason for the specific grouping of the animals is that the cytochemistry was run through in parallel, three animals at a time through all the identical fixatives, staining, and light absorption measurements. The picture is consistent within groups, but we are not confident that we can compare between groups.

We have been surprised at the very marked reduction of the RNA in the rat retina after dark rearing. After ninety days in darkness from birth, which is a fairly long time in the rat life, ganglion cell RNA concentration was reduced to much below 30 per cent. Another group of rats that were dark-reared for ninety days and then brought into normal light for sixty days recovered approximately half of the depleted RNA (Rasch *et al.,* 1961).

Reduction of RNA concentration has also been observed in the bipolar and receptor cells of cats kept in darkness. According to some work done on rabbits by Brattgård (1952), RNA differences can be statistically demonstrated in a short time, within ten minutes; more marked effects appear in thirty minutes. We have recently done some work with labeled cytidine incorporation in the ganglion cells of normal amphibians. It takes at least thirty minutes for that

TABLE 3: RNA Concentration of Retinal Ganglion Cells from Normal and Dark-reared Cats

| | | | Mean RNA-Azure B Concentration | | |
| | | | | | T-test (from control) |
Animal	Treatment	Age in Mos.	E/μ	No. of cells	
RC 1	Light-reared	36	0.255 ± 0.024	10	
RC 3	1 hr./day light	36	0.144 ± 0.010	12	3.1
RC 5	Dark-reared	36	0.109 ± 0.019	10	5.5
RC 2	Light-reared	36	0.234 ± 0.020	12	
RC 4	1 hr./day light	36	0.156 ± 0.011	10	3.4
RC 6	Dark-reared	36	0.132 ± 0.010	10	4.6
NL	Light-reared	19	0.138 ± 0.015	10	
PR	1 hr./day light	19	0.090 ± 0.012	10	2.5
GH	Dark-reared	19	0.080 ± 0.010	10	3.2
FC	Light-reared	?	0.226 ± 0.017	10	
FT	Dark-reared	40	0.164 ± 0.015	10	2.7
108	Light-reared	6	0.202 ± 0.028	10	
61	Dark-reared	3.5	$0.101 + 0.011$	10	3.4

NOTE: E/μ = optical density per micron of section thickness.

SOURCE: Modified from Rasch *et al.,* 1961.

organism to show a difference under stimulation, as opposed to non-stimulation, in darkness. We think that we have here a measure of the rate of protein turnover. This RNA depletion is a rather gross demonstration that the metabolism varies with the rate of stimulation. According to some earlier studies (Carlson, 1902; Hydén, 1960) one can overdo the stimulation and cut down protein incorporation. We have not tried to duplicate those studies as yet, but are taking them more seriously than many of us did earlier. The protein metabolism is intimately related to the rate of neural activity, and excessive demands may interfere with incorporation of RNA into cell structures.

There is at least one study (Edström and Eichner, 1958) indicating that the motivation regulating nuclei of the hypothalamus can respond by cellular changes when one changes the amount of salt intake, thereby altering the level of stimulation. The work in Scandinavia (Hamberger and Hydén, 1949) using rotation of rabbits to alter cells of Deiter's nucleus of the vestibular system is well known. These studies indicate that the short-term changes following understimulation are not confined to the visual system. Presumably the long-term and chronic effects of understimulation can also be duplicated in some nonvisual systems.

In conclusion, it appears that there is much evidence in support of the four hypotheses stated earlier. The first two are on very safe grounds, and I hardly need repeat them. The third—that the structural integrity of the nerve cells requires function—we are still hoping to document more firmly. But the metabolic demands exerted by function can be demonstrated in both short-term and long-term functional programs. Finally, an hypothesis whose generality we still have to examine much more thoroughly is that severe disuse may result in the death of some large cells of the nervous system. We may tentatively conclude that brain cells, like muscle cells, are dependent upon exercise.

REFERENCES

AARONS, L., HALASZ, H. K., & RIESEN, A. H. Interocular transfer of visual intensity discrimination after ablation of striate cortex in dark-reared kittens. *J. comp. physiol. Psychol.*, 1963, **56**, 196–199.

AXELROD, S. Effects of early blindness: performance of blind and sighted children on tactile and auditory tasks. Amer. Foundation for the Blind, Res. Ser., 1959, No. 7.

BAXTER, B. L., & RIESEN, A. H. Electro-retinogram of the visually deprived cat. *Science*, 1961, **132**, 1626–1627.

BRATTGÅRD, S. O. The importance of adequate stimulation for the chemical composition of retinal ganglion cells during early postnatal development. *Acta radiol. Suppl.,* 1952, **96**, 1–80.

BROWN, K. T., & WATANABE, K. Isolation and identification of a receptor potential from the pure cone fovea of the monkey retina. *Nature,* London, 1962, **193**, 958–960.

CARLSON, A. J. Changes in the Nissl's substance of the ganglion and the bipolar cells of the retina of the Brandt Cornorant . . . during prolonged normal stimulation. *Amer. J. Anatomy,* 1902–3, **2**, 341–347.

CHOW, K. L., & NISSEN, H. W. Interocular transfer of learning in visually naive and experienced chimpanzees. *J. comp. physiol. Psychol.,* 1955, **48**, 229–237.

CHOW, K. L., RIESEN, A. H., & NEWELL, F. W. Degeneration of retinal ganglion cells in infant chimpanzees reared in darkness. *J. comp. Neurol.,* 1957, **107**, 27–42.

COOK, W. H., WALKER, J. H., & BARR, M. L. A cytological study of trans-neuronal atrophy in the cat and rabbit. *J. comp. Neurol.,* 1951, **94**, 267–292.

EDSTRÖM, J. E., & EICHNER, D. Quantitative Ribonuklein-säureuntersuchen an den Ganglienzellen des Nucleus Supraopticus der Albino-Ratte unter experimentellen Bedingungen (Kochsalzbelastung). *Z. Zellforsch. u. mikroskop. Anat.,* 1958, **48**, 187–200.

FOLEY, J. P. First year development of a rhesus monkey (*Macaca mulatta*) reared in isolation. *J. genet. Psychol.,* 1934, **45**, 39–105.

GANZ, L., & RIESEN, A. H. Stimulus generalization to hue in the dark-reared macaque, *J. comp. physiol. Psychol.,* 1962, **55**, 92–99.

HAMBERGER, C. A., & HYDÉN, H. Production of nucleoproteins in the vestibular ganglion. *Acta oto-laryng.* Suppl. 75, 1949, 53–81.

HELD, R., & HEIN, A. Movement produced stimulation in the development of visually guided behavior. *J. comp. physiol. Psychol.,* 1963, **56**, 872–876.

HINES, M. The development and regression of reflexes, postures, and progression in the young macaque. *Carnegie Inst. Wash. Contrib. to Embryol.,* 1942, **30** (196), 153–209.

HYDÉN, H. The neuron. In J. Brachet and A. E. Mirsky (Eds.), *The cell.* New York: Academic Press, 1960. Vol. IV. Pp. 215–323.

JONES, W. H., & THOMAS, D. B. Changes in the dendritic organization of neurons in the cerebral cortex following deafferentation. *J. Anat.,* London, 1962, **96**, 375–381.

KUPFER, C., & PALMER, PATRICIA. Lateral geniculate nucleus: histological and cytochemical changes following afferent denervation and visual deprivation. *Exper. Neurol.,* 1964, **9**, 400–409.

LASHLEY, K. S., & WATSON, J. B. Notes on the development of a young monkey. *J. Anim. Behav.,* 1913, **3**, 114–139.

LEVI-MONTALCINI, RITA. Growth control of nerve cells by a protein factor and its antiserum. *Science,* 1964, **145**, 105–110.

McGINNIS, J. M. Eye-movements and optic nystagmus in early infancy. *Genet. Psychol. Monogr.,* 1930, **8**, 321–430.

ORDY, J. M., MASSOPUST, L. C., & WOLIN, L. R. Postnatal development of the retina, ERG, and acuity in the rhesus monkey. *Exp. Neurol.,* 1962, **5**, 364–382.

RASCH, ELLEN, SWIFT, H., RIESEN, A. H., & CHOW, K. L. Altered structure and composition of retinal cells in dark-reared mammals. *Exper. Cell Research,* 1961, **25**, 348–363.

RIESEN, A. H. Stimulation as a requirement for growth and function. In D. W. Fiske and S. R. Maddi, *Functions of varied experience.* Homewood, Ill.: Dorsey Press, 1961.

RIESEN, A. H., & AARONS, L. Visual movement and intensity discrimination in cats after early deprivation of pattern vision. *J. comp. physiol. Psychol.,* 1959, **52**, 142–149.

RIESEN, A. H., & MELLINGER, JEANNE C. Interocular transfer of habits in cats after alternating monocular visual experience. *J. comp. physiol. Psychol.,* 1956, **49**, 516–520.

RIESEN, A. H., RAMSEY, R. L., & WILSON, P. D. The development of visual acuity in rhesus monkeys deprived of patterned light during early infancy. *Psychonomic Science,* 1964, **1**, 33–34.

SPERRY, R. W. Cerebral organization and behavior. *Science,* 1961, **133**, 1749– √ 1757.

WALK, R. D., & GIBSON, ELEANOR J. A comparative and analytical study of visual depth perception. *Psychol. Monogr.,* 1961, **75** (15), 1–44.

WILSON, PAUL D. Visual development in rhesus monkeys neonatally deprived of patterned light. Unpublished doctoral dissertation, Univer. of Chicago, 1964.

ZIMMERMANN, R. R. Analysis of discrimination learning capacities in the infant rhesus monkey. *J. comp. physiol. Psychol.,* 1961, **54**, 1–10.

5

INDUCED MENTAL AND SOCIAL DEFICITS IN RHESUS MONKEYS

Harry F. Harlow and Gary Griffin

In the past few years we have been studying the effects of induced biochemical errors of metabolism, and even though I am going to discuss primarily a different topic I will briefly outline our information from these studies.[1] Dr. Harry Waisman has been concerned with the biochemical aspects of phenylketonuria, and we have developed relatively simple techniques for producing this condition (Waisman and Harlow, 1965). Behavioral testing reveals that these animals suffer from a severe learning loss. We have tested hundreds of normal monkeys and have never seen an idiot monkey. We have to be human to be an inborn idiot. However, practically all of our neonatal monkeys raised from birth on a high L-phenylalanine diet develop a very profound mental retardation. They do not recover intellectually after they have been on this diet for two years. Preliminary data suggest that they do not recover even after shorter periods of this dietary regimen, and that probably the first six months of life represent the minimal period required to produce a learning loss.

Many other so-called biochemical errors of metabolism may be induced artificially in the neonatal monkey. As the monkeys grow

HARRY F. HARLOW, Ph.D., is professor of psychology, University of Wisconsin. Gary Griffin is a research assistant, Department of Psychology, University of Wisconsin.

[1] This research was supported by funds supplied by grants MH–04528 and FR–00167 from the National Institutes of Health, to the University of Wisconsin Primate Laboratory and Regional Primate Research Center, respectively.

older it becomes progressively more difficult to overpower their enzyme systems. We have had some success in producing galactosemia, although we have studied only a few galactosemic animals; at least some of these monkeys later recovered full learning ability. We have been very successful in producing "maple-syrup-urine" disease by flooding the macaque monkeys' enzyme systems with valine, leucine, and isoleucine. These procedures produce very severe mental retardation, and it becomes difficult to even adapt the subjects to learning situations. Also, we have flooded monkeys with tryptophane but this does not produce serious mental retardation. My guess is that it is possible to choose many of these syndromes that depend upon some biochemical error of amino acid metabolism and reproduce them or simulate them in the laboratory by feeding the monkeys overdoses of an appropriate amino acid every four hours, twenty-four hours a day, seven days a week.

We have unpublished data that show induced phenylketonuria not only produces severe mental retardation, but also debases the infant monkey's play patterns. We are convinced that primate infants must learn to play early in life if they are ever to develop normal social-sexual lives. Play is the way in which primates socialize and develop age-mate or peer affection. In the case of the PKU monkeys, play is reduced to an infantile form, in keeping with the fact that these monkeys also suffer intellectual loss. An animal that suffers grave intellectual loss will also show loss in the allied mechanism of play. As far as we can see, one can produce many biochemical errors or simulate them and obtain a very complete, appropriate syndrome that includes severe and probably permanent intellectual retardation, as well as disruption of capabilities to form effective social integrations. But induced biochemical errors of metabolism are by no means the only factors influencing socialization in primates.

There are three primary differences between a newborn monkey and a human neonate: first is the fact that the newborn monkey is anatomically about one year of human age at birth; second, for many, though not all functions, the monkey matures about four times as fast as the human being; and third, unless you are hopelessly prejudiced, the neonatal monkey is infinitely cuter than the neonatal human being. Many of our researches on the process of socialization depend upon our capability of producing baby monkeys at will—our will, not theirs—separating them from their mothers at birth, and studying their development.

Early Infant Socialization. Early socialization in the macaque is greatly facilitated by the presence of a maternal figure that guards the infant against the threats of the external world and provides the the infant with a stable source of security and trust. Basic security in the adequately mothered human child develops during the first six to eight months of life; basic social security for the monkey develops during the first two to four months. This basic social security aids the infant in exploring its physical environment and interacting with age-mates if they are present.

Maternal security is particularly important for infant monkeys because most do not have a specific father to defend them. The monkey, like nearly all primates, is not monogamous; thus most families are matriarchal. So far as I know, there is only one primate other than man that is monogamous, and that is the gibbon. The gibbon is a low-level anthropoid ape, reputed to be totally monogamous and unbelievably stupid. Most monkey males are not family men. They usually play the role of a generalized father, protecting all members of the social group, tribe, or clan against external enemies. Occasionally a monkey male will play a maternal role and adopt a one- or two-year-old infant, in which case, I am sure, the monkey then obtains basic security from a male instead of a female.

We have known for some years that infant monkeys develop a feeling of security from surrogate mothers. Indeed, they can develop as strong a feeling of basic security from a cloth surrogate mother as they can from a real mother. However, baby monkeys obtain little security from a non-contact-giving wire surrogate mother. Figure 1 shows a baby monkey that has been raised in a dual surrogate situation (a nursing wire mother and a nonnursing cloth mother) and demonstrates that security contact is directed to the cloth mother. One might say that this figure proves the fact that you can have your cake and eat it too—if you are bright enough.

Our initial social playroom situation is illustrated in Figure 2. It has been a very effective test situation for tracing the development of peer affection. In the playroom we can trace the development of normal infant affection and also trace the debilitating effects of various kinds of abnormal early social experience. Infant monkeys that were raised on cloth surrogates and tested twenty minutes a day in the social playroom move freely about in this environment, even though they are too young to intimately interact with each other. The security of these cloth-mother-raised infants, when cloth surrogates are present, contrasts with that of an infant monkey raised from

Fᴵɢ. 1: Responsiveness of infant rhesus to cloth and wire
surrogate mothers.

birth onward on a lactating wire surrogate. The wire mother,
inanimate or animate, cannot give its infant basic security. A wire
surrogate gives its baby everything it can—its body, its bones, its
blood, and its brains, but no wire mother can give its baby love and
security.

As we have already indicated, maternal security aids the infant in
social adjustment to age-mate companions. We have studies tracing
the early social adjustments that develop through patterns of play,
not only in our playroom situation but also in our playpen situation
illustrated in Figure 3. The test situation consists of four living
cages, each housing either a mother or a mother surrogate and its
infant. The infant is free to leave its mother whenever the infant and
the mother so desire and enter a playpen unit, but the mother cannot
follow. For two hours a day the restraining barriers between the
playpen units are raised and the infants are free to interact with each

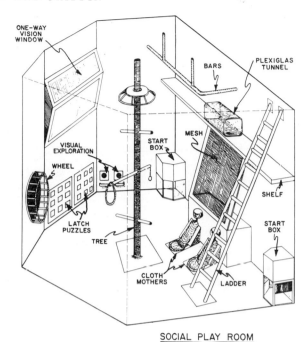

SOCIAL PLAY ROOM

Fig. 2: Social playroom situation.

other, either in pairs or in groups of four. Figure 4 shows an infant agonizing as to whether or not to leave the mother and go out and explore. From approximately thirty days of age onward, the infants will spend much of their time totally free from the mother while playing with other infants.

Development of Age-Mate or Peer Affection. We are quite convinced that peer affection, the affection for age-mates, is basically dependent upon play whether you are a monkey or a man. There is nothing mysterious about play. A monkey or a human infant who has age-mates available will automatically play with them. The play will become increasingly more complex with maturation. Play is no more unusual or surprising than prehension or locomotion. Play is relatively complex behavior that emerges inevitably when adequate external stimulation is provided (Harlow, 1962a).

An early play pattern consists of rough-and-tumble play. The monkeys wrestle, roll, and sham bite, but don't get hurt during these infantile tussles. In a second pattern of play, called noncontact play,

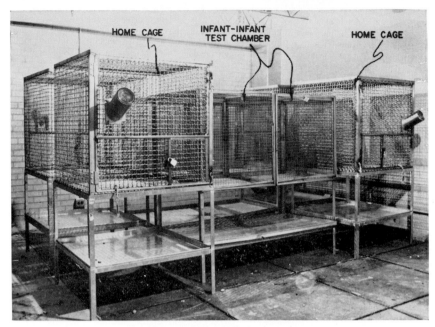

FIG. 3: Playpen situation.

the monkeys chase each other, move back and forth and up and down
in a minimum of body contact. Even though the latter is probably
more complex, these two play patterns overlap during development
and are frequently intermixed. As a matter of fact, rough-and-tumble
play tends to be a masculine play pattern in both monkeys and human
beings, and noncontact play tends to be a feminine play pattern.
The various play patterns lead to both social acceptance and social role
among infant monkeys, including sex role and dominance role. A
monkey or a human being is either going to develop these basic roles
in childhood or probably become a social discard.

Another type of social interaction pattern in monkeys is grooming.
Grooming is a very basic social pattern, probably far more important
to monkeys than to human beings. Collaborative aggression is another
interesting pattern of social interaction we have observed occasionally.
Many preadolescent monkeys learn to aggress in a co-operative
manner. Monkeys are rather feeble animals compared to leopards
and lions. If they had not learned to co-operatively aggress, there
would be no monkeys in the world and consequently no human
beings. Monkeys either co-operate or become leopard food. Two

FIG. 4: Beginning of infant independence.

infant monkeys are shown in Figure 5 in the playpen situation ag-
gressing against a mother, not their own. Monkey mothers aggress
against infants, not their own. When a monkey mother sees her infant
playing roughhouse games with other baby monkeys, with that feminine intuition that characterizes all mothers, she automatically knows
who started the fight and she lies back until the other infant comes
within arm's reach, and then she knocks him head-over-heels. The
baby monkeys do not appreciate this behavior and when they become
older they gang-up against the other monkeys' mothers, never against
their own. They aggress effectively and co-operatively against these
other mothers. They line up in the playpen unit near the other
mother and when she reaches out to grab one, the infant farthest away
reaches in the living cage with both hands and comes out with two
handsful of monkey mother hair.

We have been fascinated by such co-ordinated co-operative behavior

Fig. 5: Infant aggression against mother, not their own (mother was out of camera range).

exhibited by another group of monkeys. These monkeys lived together for a summer on a monkey island and developed strong infant-peer affectional responses. In the moat surrounding the island was a group of nice "friendly" four- to six-foot-long alligators. The monkeys would line up on the side of the moat and wait until one of these poor innocent little Florida alligators swam beside them. Two monkeys then reached down and grabbed the alligator's forelimbs and two monkeys reached down and grabbed the alligator's hind limbs and pulled the alligator flat against the cement walls where it was helpless. Other monkeys then converged and chewed on it. The alligator regarded this behavior as rather unfriendly, but I think it illustrates that monkey infants do develop strong affectional relationships for their peers in social groups and utilize these affectional relationships effectively.

As our researches have developed, we have been increasingly impressed with basic behavioral differences between male and female infant monkeys when all cultural factors were ruled out, as by raising the infants on inanimate surrogate mothers. No matter what appears in psychology or sociology books, males from birth onward are males, and females from birth onward are females. Males threaten males and females. Females may occasionally threaten females, but females do not threaten males. Threatening is a male, not female, pattern and prerogative. Conversely, females develop characteristic patterns of passivity and rigidity. When the male approaches, the female freezes and averts its face; staring at another animal's face is a threat. Threatening, passivity, and rigidity are not primary sex patterns, but are patterns upon which primary sex patterns are subsequently based. We have been so impressed by early sex differences that we believe there is not one, but rather two species of human beings; one is man and the other is woman. I can define these two species for you: man is the only animal capable of speaking, and woman is the only animal incapable of not speaking. hssss!

Boys and girls at a third-grade picnic act exactly like monkeys. The boys chase the girls and the boys chase other boys. The girls, unless *not true* acting contrary to their sex role, do not chase the boys. The boys fight and hit; the girls do not fight and hit. Instead, the girls sit on the sidelines saying mean, catty things about other little girls because they were born perfect ladies. A normal female monkey, long before she has become an adolescent, has an enormous urge to put her *false* hands on a baby monkey's body. This has been described by field investigators (DeVore, 1963) and by laboratory investigators.[2] A male monkey could not care less. To a female, babies naturally feel good.

There are two basic behavioral differences between the human male and female. The male is physically twice as strong as the female; the female, however, is more verbally gifted and she remains more verbally gifted throughout life. So when men become angry with their wives, what do they do? They argue with them! They achieve nothing and it serves them right.

Female rhesus monkeys typically attain sexual maturity during the third year, as indicated by stable ovulatory and menstrual cycles. The male monkey becomes sexually mature between four and five years of age or later, depending on the criteria used. However, most of our behavioral data indicate that monkeys either demonstrate normal adult heterosexual behavior patterns by the second year of life or they are in desperate trouble, particularly the males. I do not think these data completely generalize to human beings, even if you multiply age by four. Early infantile patterns of sexual behaviors by monkeys during the first year are often very much like abnormal adult patterns. The female responds passively to the male's approach, often by

[2] L. A. Rosenblum, personal communication.

sitting on the floor and staring into space. The male approaches the
female, grasps her body and thrusts, but his orientation to her is
random, usually involving head-clasping or body-clasping and lateral
thrusting. Through the operation and interaction of basic sex patterns and learning, more effective body orientations are gradually
achieved. Monkeys, whether raised by real mothers or surrogate
mothers, show normal heterosexual behavior if they have been
afforded ample opportunity to develop affection for peers. Most of
our monkeys, both males and females, raised in the laboratory but
provided adequate peer experience from infancy onward, either in the
playroom or playpen situations, exhibited normal adult-type heterosexual posturing during their second year of laboratory life. Such
behavior is illustrated in Figure 6, which shows the female posturing

Fig. 6: Normal adult male and female sex posture.

with tail erect, buttocks erect, hind legs extended, and forelimbs flexed, looking backward at the male. It also shows the normal male pattern of dorsoventral mounting, with the male clasping the buttocks of the female with his hands and clasping her legs with a double-foot clasp.

Maternal Behavior. Another basic affectional social pattern that depends on early peer affectional development is that of adequate maternal behavior. The normal macaque maternal pattern is illustrated in Figure 7 with the infant loosely encircled in the mother's arms. The reciprocal infant pattern involves manual maternal contact with the infant holding the mother's nipple in its mouth. This is probably an example of nonnutritive sucking and we are convinced that this response is simply a component of the total contact-clinging pattern that we previously described (Harlow, 1960).

FIG. 7: Normal maternal response to macaque infant.

We have conducted a series of experiments to determine the minimal requirements of effective motherhood. To test the effect of previous specific infantile experience on maternal efficiency, we compared maternal efficiency between primiparous and multiparous mothers and found few significant group differences with our measures. For most test scores there were no group differences, as illustrated by Figure 8. Basically, both primiparous and multiparous female monkeys turned out to be very efficient infant-raising mechanisms. Apparently an infant monkey is an innate releasing mechanism for monkey maternal female behavior, if the females have enjoyed adequate earlier peer affectional experience. I am sure that human beings are more complicated than monkeys. Although monkey infants are consistently demanding, some human babies are apparently not very demanding and are not very effective feedback mechanisms to their mothers. However, it appears that most primate females are good mothers.

One of the few significant differences we found between the multi-

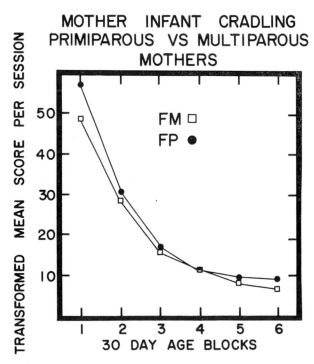

Fig. 8: Cradle scores by primiparous and multiparous macaque mothers.

parous and the primiparous females was the time of appearance of the ambivalent or transitional maternal stage, the stage at which the monkey mother begins to mildly punish and reject her infant, with or without obvious provocation (Harlow, Harlow, and Hansen, 1963). I am certain that this developmental stage releases an automatic mechanism by which the monkey mother starts the difficult process of separating the infant from herself. The affection of the infant for the mother is so totally overwhelming that infants, at least most primate infants, cannot spontaneously separate themselves from their mothers. Probably this effect is true for both monkey and human infants, and it is the obligation of every primate mother to begin to psychologically separate the child from herself at an appropriate stage. The multiparous mothers punished their babies earlier than the primiparous mothers, i.e., the primiparous mothers were loving but unknowledgeable.

Effects of Social Isolation on Social Development. For a long period of time we have been conducting studies on various kinds of social deprivation. Two types that have been investigated are partial and total social deprivation.

If we raise infant monkeys under conditions of partial social isolation, most of them eventually show patterns of deviant behavior. One of these patterns is persistent nonnutritional orality usually directed toward the pollex or hallux. A second pattern that many semisocially isolated monkeys show is one that we have called the autistic pattern of clutching the body and head by the arms and legs and violently rocking back and forth. A third pattern is that of simply staring vacantly into space, paying little attention to people or other monkeys. A fourth pattern is that of repeatedly circling the cage from side to side or from top to bottom. At a zoo we frequently see this behavior in caged animals unless they are raised in a family group. The big cats can often be observed engaging in this stereotyped pacing. A fifth pattern seen in many but not all partially isolated monkeys is self-aggression, or if you prefer to use a psychological term, intrapunitive aggression. This is illustrated by the monkey in Figure 9, which is chewing on its own arm. We do not understand the origin or significance of this pattern. It is usually seen in monkeys that have been subjected to prolonged partial social isolation.

Monkeys subjected to partial social isolation, probably for six months, and almost certainly for one year, do not, even when given the opportunity, develop adequate play responses with age-mates or

FIG. 9: Self-aggression by macaque monkey.

peers. In other words, prolonged social isolation destroys effective age-mate interaction, and once age-mate interaction is eliminated, so are most heterosexual behaviors. We encountered a dramatic illustration of the effect of early semisocial isolation on social-sexual behavior about four years ago. Ten males and ten females that were raised in semisocial isolation for three years would not breed in the laboratory. So in desperation we put them on the monkey island in Madison's Vilas Park Zoo. On the island they adjusted fairly rapidly. They formed friendship patterns and groomed each other within the first week. Once they started grooming we thought it would be just a matter of time before all other behaviors would appear. We were sure that some summer evening a full moon would rise over the waters of Lake Wingra, the wind would waft its fragrant fairy fingers through the leaves of the trees, and that stimulated thusly, the males and females would do something other than just seeing eye to eye. The monkeys were left on the island for two and a half months. Although grooming and some play developed, nothing was achieved in terms of normal heterosexual behavior.

By techniques that have already been described (Harlow, 1962b), a number of female monkeys that had had no peer experience during the first eighteen months of life were eventually impregnated. We call these motherless mothers. They were mothers that had been separated from their mothers at birth and also had had no opportunity to develop affection for age-mate members of their species during the first year of life. By an incredible twist of fate, our first four motherless mothers gave birth to babies within a twenty-five day span. We put the four mothers and their infants in a playpen situation. All of these mothers were totally inadequate, and two of the first four motherless mothers almost killed their infants (Seay, Alexander, and Harlow, 1964). As a matter of fact, three subsequent motherless mothers, not reported in detail here, did kill their infants. None of the infants would have survived had we not hand-cared for them. The mothers tended to follow a pattern of maternal indifference, illustrated in Figure 10, though all of them were brutal at times. This infant monkey appears to be looking up at its mother and saying, "How in God's name did I ever rate a mother like you?" This mother is totally indifferent. But regardless of maternal indifference or brutality, the infants tried repeatedly and determinedly to make maternal contact, day after day, and week after week. As a matter of fact, the infants were so persistent that most of the mothers gave up resisting their advances from about four months onward, except for occasional outbursts of rejection or abuse.

You may have read in a psychology or physiology book that pain is prepotent over any other stimulus. Infant affection appears to be totally prepotent over any pain inflicted by the mother. The mothers could beat the infants to the point of death but the infants would keep on returning, simply for the opportunity to touch some part of the mother's body. The baby's affection for the mother is deep, enduring, and almost unbelievably strong. There are any number of human cases of drunken parents who have beaten their children senseless; social workers separate these children from their mothers, but after a few days the children desperately want to return to their mothers.

At the present time we are also studying the effects of total social isolation on the social development of monkeys. Since monkeys can

Fig. 10: Maternal indifference by motherless mother monkey.

be socially crippled by partial social isolation, and since total social isolation is seldom seen in human beings, one might wonder why we are interested in total social isolation. With total social isolation we can produce all the effects of partial social isolation and obtain these effects more rapidly and probably to a more devasting extent. *wonderfu*

Total social deprivation involves separating the baby monkey from its mother six hours after birth and raising it in a stainless steel cage in which it never sees any other animal, monkey or human, for a three-, six-, or twelve-month period (Rowland, 1964). During this time the animals can be tested under total social isolation for their learning capability by remote control devices built into the isolation cages. An infant monkey photographed immediately after six months of social isolation, while still in its isolation chamber, is shown in Figure 11. Monkeys raised under conditions of total social isolation for six months are probably totally socially destroyed. Sex behavior is so inhibited that the monkeys not only fail to show normal heterosexual behaviors, but they show great depression of autoerotic behaviors. Six months of total social isolation has debilitating effects on play and threat patterns. Both of these patterns are greatly delayed and depressed, with isolates showing absolutely no play with normal controls and no threats toward them.

Although the six-month isolated monkeys appear to be hopelessly socially crippled, the effects of twelve months of total social isolation are apparently even more devastating. There is no rudimentary self-play or social play and simple curiosity is greatly depressed. There is no positive interaction whatsoever between the isolates and control monkeys, and the isolates are helpless when the control monkeys aggress against them. After removing them from the isolation chamber we gradually adapted our isolated monkeys to the Wisconsin General Test Apparatus (WGTA) (Harlow, 1949) and to a shuttle-

FIG. 11: Macaque response after six months of total social isolation.

box (Rowland, 1964) and found to our surprise that there was no indication of any learning loss, either discrimination learning, delayed response learning, learning set formation, or shock avoidance. One of the most complex learning tasks is six-trial discrimination learning set. Intraproblem learning is represented in Figure 12. This shows the performance for trials 2–6 on problems 301–400. The interproblem learning curves, in Figure 13, are based on the per cent correct response on trials 2–6 for blocks of 100 problems. Such differences that appear probably relate to the difficulty in adapting the isolate animals. No significant differences were found between groups and there is no indication of any permanent learning impairment. It should be noted that these isolated monkeys had some learning experience while under total social deprivation (Rowland, 1964).

We know these data are different from dog data obtained in Canada (Thompson and Heron, 1954) and a wealth of rat data obtained in the United States (Woods, Ruckelshaus, and Bowling, 1960). Furthermore, the monkey learning data appear to be unlike the human clinical data—or are they? It is possible that the schizophrenic

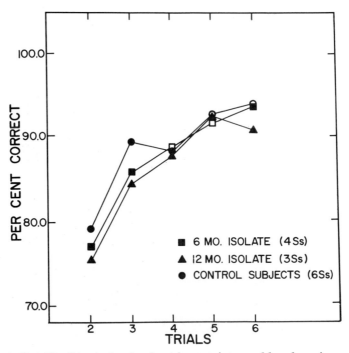

Fig. 12: Discrimination learning set, intraproblem learning.

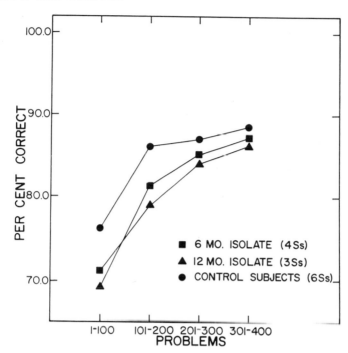

Fɪɢ. 13: Discrimination learning set, interproblem learning.

or autistic child shows gross intellectual deficit because he cannot make effective social communication. He does not learn language because he isolates himself from both peers and adults, and consequently, when tested on the Stanford-Binet or even a "nonlanguage" test, he performs very poorly. But basically, if we wish to trust the monkey data, there is the suggestion that there was no real permanent intellectual loss when the animal's intellectual capability was measured in the above situations.

REFERENCES

DᴇVoʀᴇ, I. Mother-infant relations in free-ranging baboons. In H. L. Rheingold (Ed.), *Maternal behavior in mammals.* New York: Wiley, 1963.

Hᴀʀʟᴏᴡ, H. F. The formation of learning sets. *Psychol. Rev.,* 1949, **56,** 51–65.

———. Primary affectional patterns in primates. *Amer. J. Orthopsychiat.,* 1960, **30,** 676–684,

――. Development of the second and third affectional systems in macaque monkeys. In T. T. Tourlentes, S. L. Pollack, & H. E. Himwich (Eds.), *Research approaches to psychiatric problems: a symposium.* New York: Grune & Stratton, 1962a. Pp. 209–229.

――. The heterosexual affectional system in monkeys. *Amer. Psychologist,* 1962b, **17**, 1–9.

HARLOW, H. F., HARLOW, M. K., & HANSEN, E. W. The maternal affectional system of rhesus monkeys. In H. L. Rheingold (Ed.), *Maternal behavior in mammals.* New York: Wiley, 1963. Pp. 354–381.

ROWLAND, G. L. The effect of total social isolation upon learning and social behavior in rhesus monkeys. Unpublished doctoral dissertation, Univer. of Wisconsin, 1964.

SEAY, B., ALEXANDER, B., & HARLOW, H. F. The maternal behavior of socially deprived rhesus monkeys. *J. abnorm. soc. Psychol.,* in press.

THOMPSON, W. R., & HERON, W. The effects of restricting early experience on the problem solving capacity of dogs. *Canad. J. Psychol.,* 1954, **8**, 17–31.

WAISMAN, H. A., & HARLOW, H. F. Experimental phenylketonuria in infant monkeys. *Science,* 1965, **147**, 685–695.

WOODS, D. J., RUCKELSHAUS, S. I., & BOWLING, D. M. Some effects of free (and restricted) environmental rearing conditions upon the adult behavior in the rat. *Psychol. Rep.,* 1960, **6**, 191–200.

6

LEARNING PROCESSES OF THE MENTALLY RETARDED

David Zeaman

The experimental psychologist may attack retardation in at least two ways: (1) find the laws, principles, or regularities that govern the behavior of retardates; or (2) find the *unique* laws of retardate behavior, that is, those ways of behaving which characterize people of low IQ, and them alone.

Of these two possibilities (find laws, find unique laws), my wife (Dr. B. J. House) and I have pursued the first with some modest success, but we are frequently faulted by impatient critics for not doing the second.

Whenever we present descriptions of some regularities in the problem-solving of retarded children, then with the inevitability of death (or taxes), the criticism will be made that our findings (or theory) are *not unique*. The argument takes several forms, sometimes the seemingly innocuous query: "But what has all you have said got to do with retardation?"—and sometimes the not so subtle, personal attack: "You are just using retardates for your *own theoretical purposes.*" This is to be read "evil theoretical purposes."

After having spent ten years in the laboratory experimenting almost exclusively with retardates, Dr. House and I began to wonder if there were not some cognitive content to the charges that deserved formal reply. Washed clean of emotion, the criticism amounts to a request for *unique* laws—for IQ-specific laws.

David Zeaman, Ph.D., is professor of psychology, University of Connecticut.

To establish unique laws, one must show that a particular behavioral property is not shared by any other class of subjects. For example, we have a theory and much experimental evidence to show that the deficiency shown by moderately retarded children in learning to discriminate between simple stimuli, such as a blue square and a red circle, is the result not of slow learning, as one might expect, but rather inattention—initial inattention to the relevant aspect of the stimuli. Is this unique? To find the answer, we must do research with other subjects, normal children of equal mental ages, or other species of comparable developmental level, or humans with other pathologies than retardation. In short, we must undertake a giant program of comparative psychology, manipulating ontogenetic, phylogenetic, or pathological factors. Paradoxically this would take us out of our retardate laboratory and lay us open to the very criticism we were seeking to answer. "What are you doing with monkeys, kindergarteners, rats, and psychotics if you *really care* about retardates?" This alone would not dissuade us from making a beginning on the giant comparative program, if there were not other problems. Control is the big one.

The modal paper of the researcher looking for the unique laws is a one-shot affair, in which retardates are compared with normal children of matched MA (mental age) or CA (chronological age). Control in such comparisons is fraught with difficulty. If you match for CA, then MA is out of control. If you match for MA, then CA is necessarily out of control. If you assume CA is not a relevant variable and match for MA, then other differences appear to be out of control. Length of institutionalization, home environments, previous schooling, tender-loving-care, and socio-economic status are factors likely to be different for retardates and normals. To arrange adequate controls for these variables (if relevant) would require heroic investigators and even more heroic budgets. Not being heroes, we have adopted the more limited but more reasonable goal: to investigate retardate behavior, and to write some part of the psychology of retardation, even if it is not unique.

If one finds some variables governing retardate behavior, even if these are traditional variables yielding expected relations, this is all to the good. The psychology of retardation must include many non-unique regularities, and research is needed to establish these. Surely, if any application of psychology in modifying the behavior of retardates is to be successful, the uniqueness of the laws is irrelevant to such a pursuit.

The behavioral engineer is interested in laws about *manipulable* independent variables, not necessarily unique laws. From the educational or engineering point of view if retardate behavior is not different in principle, just in degree, from the behavior of other subjects, so much the better. In other words, if the laws of behavior are the same, but differences in parameter values distinguish retardates (as Clark Hull postulated), this should simplify application (Hull, 1945). As everyone knows who has tried to formulate quantitative descriptions of behavioral processes, the boundaries set by free parameters are extremely broad. In order for retardate behavioral laws to be unique in form, retardate behavior would have to be very different indeed.

Needless to say, after this defensive preamble, we have chosen to ignore the requirement of unique laws, and sought instead to write a part of the psychology of retardation. To do this we study only retardates. And for our critics, we have only a single adjective. We say they are impatient. In ten years we have completed about forty experiments and left incomplete perhaps twice this number after pilot studies indicated weak effects or poor control. Most, but not all, have been in the area of visual discrimination learning. These tell us something about the retardate processes of learning, attention, and retention.

Let me summarize some of our major conclusions about the visual discrimination learning of moderately retarded, institutionalized children—most imbeciles or trainable with mental ages between two and six years—learning to distinguish between pairs of simple objects.

1. Their discrimination learning is mediated, not by verbal behavior, but by attention. For this reason we have not found the Kendlers' verbal mediation hypothesis to be useful for these subjects and problems (Kendler and Kendler, 1962). The discrimination learning of retardates does involve a chain of at least two responses, but the first is not a verbal label, but rather the response of paying attention to relevant stimulus dimensions. The second response of the chain is approaching the positive cue of the relevant dimension. In this respect, retardates are not unique.

2. Retardates, among their other troubles, have a low initial probability of paying attention to the relevant dimensions. We usually require them to look at forms and colors. They prefer to look at positions. Give them a position discrimination to solve and they solve it faster than college students, even nonretarded college students.

3. Their attention focuses, when it does, on broad classes of stimuli,

on whole dimensions, not specific cues. They attend to color, not red and green; to form, not square and triangle. Other subjects do this, too.

4. Learning and extinction, once these processes start, do not appear to be related to intelligence. For the problems we set them, learning may be complete in one trial, after they have begun to attend. Our mathematical models use a one-trial learning postulate with accurate fittings of empirical learning curves.

5. If our attention theory is correct, the poor discrimination performance of retardates is reversible, to the extent that attention can be harnessed and properly directed. This is easier than trying to teach them verbal labels for the stimuli.

6. *Approach* tendencies to *positive* cues are formed more rapidly early in learning than *avoidance* of *negative* cues. This might be interpreted to mean that acquisition is a faster process than extinction earlier in learning. Spence's theory predicts this (Spence, 1960).

7. In a well-established discrimination, approach and avoidance tendencies have approximately equal strengths.

8. The nature of stimuli provides a powerful determinant of retardate visual discrimination learning:

a) Stimulus novelty is a discriminable aspect of stimuli that can facilitate discrimination.

b) The absolute size of stimuli and figure-to-ground ratios control discrimination learning of colors and forms. The bigger the better.

c) Form is a stronger dimension than color (despite the fact that our subjects are more likely to be able to name colors than forms).

d) Some aspects of form, such as symmetry, make for good discrimination. This is true even when *information* is controlled. This should make Gestalt psychologists happy.

e) Three-dimensional figures are more easily discriminated than otherwise equivalent two-dimensional figures. This is independent of additional tactual or kinesthetic cues.

f) Relational cues (such as oddity and similarity) are exceedingly difficult for retardates; and very special training procedures are necessary to teach them how to solve these problems.

g) Redundancy facilitates. The greater the number of relevant dimensions, the greater the likelihood of learning. This appears to be a universal law of discrimination learning. A boundary condition of this law is placed by attention: redundant dimensions to which attention is not directed have no effect.

h) The greater the number of variable, irrelevant dimensions, the poorer the performance. Restle's theory of discrimination learning predicts the latter two findings (Restle, 1955).

i) Stimulus compounds of color and form are used by retardates, as well as stimulus elements, and to about equal degrees. This, unfortunately, makes Restle's theory of discrimination learning inapplicable to retardate behavior in our situations.

j) The use of both compound and component solutions increases with mental age and IQ, but these tendencies do not increase differentially. Some theorists, such as Werner (1948) and Spence (1960), have disagreed on the developmental trends in the use of stimulus compounds and components. One theorist (Werner) sees the use of compounds as more primitive, the other sees components as more primitive. Our data appear to agree with neither position.

9. Transfer operations, such as reversal and intra- and extra-dimensional shifts, are sensitive determinants of retardate visual discrimination learning. These operations not only give much information on the nature of underlying processes, they also hold out hope of successful remediation of poor discrimination performance, particularly the powerful positive transfer effects obtainable with intra-dimensional shifts. Keeping the relevant dimension constant from problem to problem helps a great deal. If, for example, attention can be focused on a stimulus dimension using easily discriminated cues of that dimension, then subsequent substitution of more difficult cues of the same dimension may lead to a ready solution of the difficult problem (House and Zeaman, 1960).

10. Reinforcements are important (we use M & M candy, and praise) in two respects but not a third. First, the stimulus properties of the reinforcement exert behavioral control. If, for example, candy reinforcement matches in color the positive cue of the discrimination problem, performance improves much faster than if it does not. This is the Jarvik effect, observed with primates (Jarvik, 1956). Secondly, the schedule of the reinforcements also exerts behavioral control. Under the partial, random schedules characteristic of probability learning experiments, our retardate subjects neither match the schedule, nor maximize, but respond between these bounds. In this respect they resemble normal children of preschool age. The amount or value of the reward does not appear to be important over a wide

range of variation. Candy satiation has no apparent effect. This implies that the satiation effects of reinforcement are weak or absent.

11. The only response factor we have investigated is the distinctiveness of responses. Proprioceptively distinctive responses to the positive and negative cues appear to help discrimination learning to a moderate degree (House, 1964).

12. Long-term retention is good, while short-term memory is very poor. A single problem learned to a strong criterion shows little or no decrement for many days. On the other hand, a problem learned to a weak criterion (in a session which includes other problems) shows loss of retention in a matter of seconds. This finding might bear on a currently controversial issue: is short-term memory the same process as long-term memory? If retardates were deficient in one but not in the other, it would suggest two processes. Unfortunately, there is also evidence for the opposite conclusion. Retroactive interference operates in the short-term memory of those subjects as it does in long-term memory in normals. The Skaggs-Robinson hypothesis appears to hold in short-term memory of retardates; as a consequence retardate data add an argument for both sides of this controversy.

13. Mental age and IQ each correlate .5 with over-all performance on visual discrimination learning. Theoretically these relations are mediated by attentional rather than associative defects. With MA and IQ controlled, diagnostic categories do not appear to have an effect.

14. We have not been able to find much evidence of learning sets in trainable retardates, after an initial problem has been solved to a strong criterion—certainly nothing like Harlow gets with monkeys, with interproblem improvement extending over hundreds of problems (Harlow, 1949).

15. We have, on the other hand, observed *failure sets*. Prolonged failure on difficult problems leads to an inability to solve even the easiest problems, ordinarily solved in a trial or two.

Having enumerated the important variables in discriminative learning, let me review some factors we have found not to be important.

1. Motivation is not important, in the sense of deprivation and satiation. The value of the incentive is a weak determinant under the conditions of our experiments.

2. Diagnostic category is an unreliable predictor of simple discriminative ability, with MA and IQ controlled.

3. There is not much variance attributed to verbal mediation. The

verbal behavior of retardates is a co-ordinate rather than a mediating system. Teaching verbal labels for discriminative cues does not result in high transfer to other instrumental (approach) responses in our experimental situation.

4. Complex trait terms or qualitative behavioral attributes of retardates, such as rigidity, distractability, or concreteness, have been of little use for the prediction or control of the behavior of these subjects.

Now let us turn to our actual experiments. For our two-choice visual discrimination experiments, we use a modified Wisconsin General Test Apparatus (WGTA) as shown in Figure 1. The main feature of this apparatus is a tray carrying two stimuli. The tray is slid out to the subject who sits in a chair at the left. The experimenter sits on the other side behind a one-way mirror and baits the stimuli (usually just one) with candy.

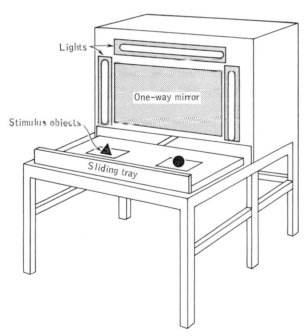

FIG. 1: Discrimination learning apparatus. (Figures for this paper are from *Handbook of Mental Deficiency* edited by Norman Ellis. Copyright © 1963 McGraw-Hill, Inc. Used by permission of McGraw-Hill Book Company.)

The procedure is standard; a correction or noncorrection procedure may be used for twenty-five trials per day in a massed sequence to a criterion of twenty correct out of twenty-five trials. If the subject does not achieve criterion after ten days of training, he is considered to have failed. The subjects are all institutionalized retardates of mixed diagnoses, almost all within the trainable or imbecile range. MA's range for the most part from two to six years, IQ's from twenty to sixty.

Typical problems of intermediate difficulty consist of objects differing in both color and form. Empirical learning curves of six groups of imbeciles learning to discriminate objects such as these are presented in Figure 2. The subjects were divided into six groups on the basis of the number of days it took them to reach criterion. Those at left took only one day to reach criterion, those at the far right took six days to learn, and the groups in between took intermediate numbers of days to learn. The family of curves generated here is ogival. The functions are similar in that they all start at chance performance and once they start to rise, they rise fast. Slope differences in the transition zones of these functions are slight. If the subjects at left are bright and the subjects at right less intelligent, then an interesting possibility is suggested. Intelligence is *not* related to learning speed, but to how long it takes for learning to start.

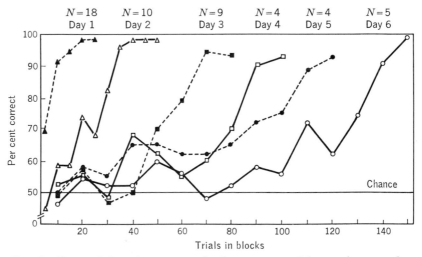

Fig. 2: Forward learning curves of sub-groups requiring various numbers of training days to reach criterion. The number of subjects in each group appears at top.

It appears to us that the length of the initial plateau representing the number of trials before learning starts is due to inattention— inattention to the relevant aspects of the stimuli. This interpretation implies that intelligence is related to attention rather than learning; duller children start out attending to the incorrect dimensions.

If the terminal points of the curves are brought together (rather than the starting points) and averaged, we get backward learning curves (Hayes, 1953). Figure 3 shows the curves of high and low MA groups, further separated into learners and nonlearners. At the left is the backward learning curve of a group of subjects with mental ages of four to six years. At the right, is the learning curve of the subjects with MA two to four. The flat functions represent the nonlearners, who perform at chance levels for both groups. The low MA group has twice as many nonlearners as the high MA group. Clearly, mental age is related to performance on this discrimination learning task—to *one specific aspect* of performance—not rate of

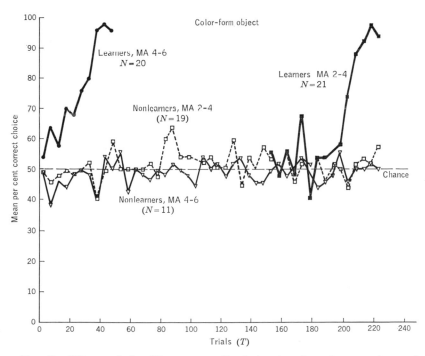

FIG. 3: Effects of intelligence on discrimination learning, as shown in the average performances of four groups classified by mental age and achievement. Backward curves are plotted for the two groups of learners.

learning, once it starts, but rather the number of trials it takes for learning to start.

We can now restate our conjecture: the difference between relatively bright and dull children among retardates is not learning ability but rather a difference in some other process providing a necessary condition for learning. Attention is such a process. Attention, or inattention, controls the length of the initial plateau, and it in turn is controlled by mental age (among other things). If our conjecture is correct, then whatever other factors control attention should also control discrimination performance. Stimuli are factors that control attention, and we show next that these are potent determinants of performance.

Consider first multidimensionally different stimuli, such as a pot cover and soap dish—often called "junk" stimuli. These have many redundant relevant dimensions; they are likely to have one that is conspicuous, or attention-getting. According to the attention theory these should be easily discriminated, and they are. They are learned almost immediately.

In contrast, two-dimensional pattern discrimination problems, even though these have at least two relevant dimensions, are difficult. Three-dimensional or stereometric equivalents of these (what we have called color-form objects) are much easier. Theoretically the greater ease of stereometric over planometric stimuli can be accounted for by the fewer number of redundant dimensions in the planometric stimuli.

In Figure 4 the rising curve at the far left is for "junk" stimuli. It represents fastest learning. Next in difficulty is color-form object, which has at least two relevant dimensions, color and form. The next rising function is that of form object, which has at least one relevant dimension, form. At the far right are curves for color-form pattern (planometric) stimuli, and for color alone in an object discrimination task. A majority of children fail pattern and color problems.

There is no question that stimulus characteristics can produce wide differences in the length of the initial plateau, but the final slopes of these functions are not widely different. It appears, therefore, that intelligence and stimuli produce similar effects. Both change the lengths of initial plateaus, and in our theory, both are related to attention to relevant dimensions.

The role of stimulus novelty also adds weight to our theoretical analyses on the role of attention. Novelty is a strong attention-getting aspect of stimuli. Introduction of novel stimuli after prolonged failure

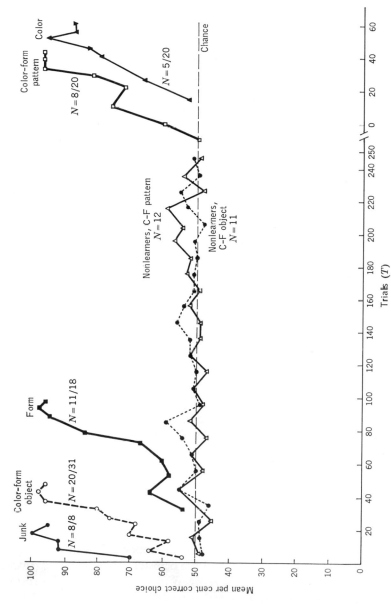

Fig. 4: Backward learning curves for the discrimination of several kinds of stimuli. Average performance levels of nonlearners stay close to chance. Numbers next to curves refer to number of successful ss and total number of ss.

can dramatically facilitate discrimination. For subjects who had been failing on a two-choice object discrimination for over a thousand trials, the introduction of a new negative stimulus was often followed by problem solution. The new negative stimulus has high attention-getting properties. The same effects are obtained by adding a novel positive stimulus, but are not obtained if both positive and negative stimuli are made novel (Zeaman, House, and Orlando, 1958).

Transfer operations are potent controllers of attention and of discrimination performance. We will discuss three types of transfer operations. Suppose that for original learning we have a color discrimination, green positive versus red negative, with form randomized. For a reversal we merely interchange the role of red and green. For an intradimensional shift, after original learning we keep color relevant, but shift to new cues, such as yellow and blue. For an extradimensional shift, the previously irrelevant form dimension is relevant, and color becomes irrelevant. The correct solution is to approach square or avoid circle.

In terms of attention theory, an extradimensional shift should be difficult. Having learned to pay attention to color, the new problem requires us to attend to form. The intradimensional shift should be easy, if attention focuses on broad classes of stimuli. Having learned in the first problem to look at color, there should be positive transfer to a new color problem because we start out attending to the relevant dimension.

The reversal shift represents a mixed case. We start out looking at the relevant dimension (which should give positive transfer), but we approach the wrong cue (which should give negative transfer). The over-all net effect will be positive or negative transfer depending upon the importance of attention. For dimensions we are very likely to look at from the beginning, attention is not important, and reversal should produce a negative transfer due to competition from the incorrect instrumental response. For dimensions initially commanding a low probability of attention, reversal should be a positive transfer condition because the original learning task trains the subject to attend to the relevant dimension.

The literature on reversals is filled with apparently contradictory results. Sometimes reversals yield positive transfer, sometimes negative. Our theory says that both should happen, depending upon the state of a third variable, attention, or the probability that the subjects will be looking at the relevant dimension at the outset of training. Since we use color and form as relevant dimensions, and these are relatively inconspicuous for retardates, reversal involving these dimensions theoretically becomes a positive transfer condition for them. And they do find these problems easy to solve.

Figure 5 shows three empirical curves: for reversal, intradimensional shift, and extradimensional shift. The easiest is intradimensional shift, the most difficult is extradimensional shift, and reversal is intermediate, but closer to intradimensional shift.

On the qualitative level, the array of data presented so far is consistent with our attention theory. To develop quantitative pre-

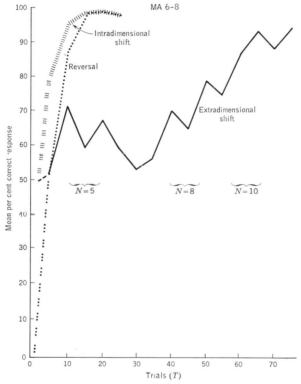

FIG. 5: Backward learning curves for three groups of retardates in the intradimensional-shift, reversal, and extradimensional-shift conditions. Mean percentages of correct choices are plotted for blocks of five trials. Broken lines connect the initial block with the starting level for each condition.

The number of subjects contributing data to various sections of the extradimensional-shift group function diminishes from ten to five.

diction, we have written a formal mathematical theory of retardate discrimination learning, similar to Wyckoff's (1952), which I will sketch in the briefest possible terms.

According to the traditional one-stage, nonchaining (single-link) theory, we begin with two discriminably different stimuli, S and S', and two responses, R and R', differing in strength or quality. A discrimination is formed when each of the stimuli is more strongly connected with one of the responses than the other.

Attention theory is more complicated than this. It posits a *chain of two responses,* with the first response, the attention response, producing the stimuli to be discriminated. The broad dimensions of stimuli, such as color and form, compete for a limited attention. Attending to a dimension enhances the cues produced by that dimension. Hence there is a chain of two responses to be learned: (1) attention and (2) instrumental approach.

Figure 6 shows three dimensions competing for attention: color, form, and some dimension n (likely to be position). If the subject is limited in attention, he will not be able to attend to all on a single trial. If the attention response to the relevant dimension (O_1) has a high probability of occurrence, the child is likely to see the cues of that dimension (triangle and square, if form is relevant). If attention is paid to an irrelevant dimension, for example, color, then the cues of that dimension will be observed.

Figure 6 can also be regarded as a probability tree of all the events that theoretically can take place on a trial. I will not dwell on its mathematical aspects, since the theory is published (Zeaman and House, 1963), but instead will point out its main features. Every branch on the tree represents a theoretical event, and associates with it a probability. Reading from left to right, the first set of branches shows the observing or attention responses competing. That is stage one. The next stage shows the two-choice possibilities that arise after attention has been paid to some dimension. The subject can make one of two instrumental responses of approach in this stage. Finally two other possibilities emerge, either the trial ends in candy reinforcement (G) or does not (G'). Such a tree enables the theorist to write an expression for the probability of a successful trial, that is, one ending in candy reinforcement. The equation is as follows:

$$P = Po_{(1)} Pr_{(1)} + \tfrac{1}{2} (1 - Po_{(1)})$$

To complete the theory, all that is necessary is a set of rules or equations that indicates how the probabilities change on every trial,

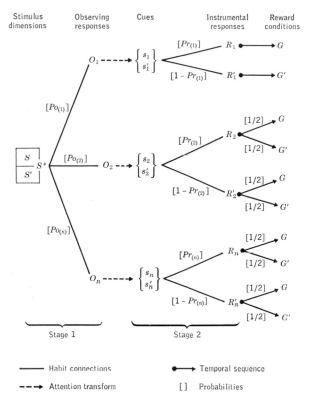

FIG. 6: Probability tree of the basic model. The branches represent all the possible events that can theoretically occur on a single trial. The probability of occurrence of each branch is written in brackets.

S: the set of relevant stimulus dimensions

S': the set of irrelevant dimensions

S^*: combined set of S and S'

O_i: attention to the ith dimension

R_i: approach to the positive cue of the ith dimension

R_i': approach to the negative cue of the ith dimension

G: reinforcement

G': nonreinforcement

depending upon whether a trial ends in a reinforcement or not. We apply an incremental or acquisition operator Q_A to the probabilities of responses occurring on trials ending in reinforcement, and a decre-

mental or extinction operator Q_E for a trial ending in nonreinforcement. The equations are

$$Q_A \text{ (Prob)} = \text{(Prob)} + \theta \text{ } (1 - \text{Prob})$$

and

$$Q_E \text{ (Prob)} = \text{(Prob)} - \theta \text{ (Prob)}.$$

These are commonly used linear operators. They operate only on the
probabilities of responses that occur on a given trial. A novel feature
of attention theory is our distributional operator. If some probability
of an observing response changes because of reward or nonreward,
the probabilities of the other, nonelicited, responses undergo indirect
changes so as to keep constant the ratios of all pairs of $Po_{(1)}$. Our
distributional operators do this for us.

The indirect acquisition operator Q_{aj} is defined by

$$Q_{aj} \text{ } (Po_{(i)} = Po_{(i)} + \frac{\theta_0 \, Po_{(i)} \, Po_{(j-)}}{1 - Po_{(j-)}},$$

and the indirect extinction operator Q_e by

$$Q_e \text{ } (Po_{(i)}) = Po_{(i)} - \frac{\theta_0 \, Po_{(i)} \, (1 - Po_{(j+)})}{1 - Po_{(j+)}} = Po_{(i)} - \theta_0 \, Po_{(i)},$$

where $Po_{(j+)}$ is the probability of the directly reinforced observing
response, and $Po_{(j-)}$ is the probability of a nonreinforced observing
response.

The probability tree in Figure 6 and these equations comprise the
mathematical heart of attention theory. Unless we give only a few
trials per problem, it is not yet possible to solve this set of equations
explicitly or to derive simple methods of parameter estimation using
the data we have on hand. It is possible, however, to have recourse
to a computer simulation of the system. Our theoretical assumptions
are fed into a digital computer, together with specific assumptions
about parameter values and starting levels of probabilities. The
computer is programmed to deduce the consequences of the general
and specific assumptions. It does this in the form of sets of changing
probabilities over trials. The computer can, also, with the help
of a table of random numbers convert predicted probabilities of a
correct response to "yes-no" decisions. Such decisions we ascribe to
"stat-children." A stat-child is thus a statistical creature that obeys the
rules of a probability model.

If the correspondence between stat-child behavior and retardate
performance is good, we infer that the theoretical postulates and

specific assumptions are valid. There is, of course, flexibility in adjustment of parameter values and starting levels; but despite the
wide boundaries allowed, the correspondence of stat-child and retardate behavior is by no means a necessary outcome. Furthermore it is
of great theoretical importance to discover *what* theoretical parameter
must be adjusted to bring about the correspondence. An illustration
of this point is given in the next two figures.

Figure 7 shows the effects on stat-child performance of variation
in the theoretical learning rate parameter, θ. If intelligence were
related to learning rate (a traditional view) this family of functions
would be predicted for groups of subjects differing in intelligence.
Figures 2 and 3 indicate that the observed retardate functions do not
match these stat-children predictions; we therefore reject the notion
that intelligence is related to discrimination learning rate (θ) under
the conditions of our experiments.

Figure 8 shows a family of stat-children functions representing
differences in initial probability ($Po_{(1,0)}$) of attending to the relevant
dimension. This family resembles the retardate data of Figures 2
and 3, and lends empirical weight to our basic proposition: that the

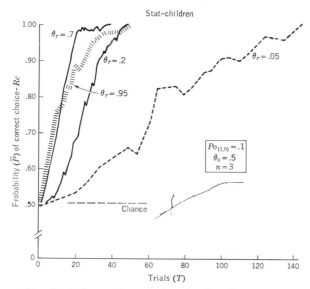

Fig. 7: Effects of variation in θ_0, the parameter
controlling rate of learning of the observing responses
O_i. Variation in θ_r, the instrumental learning rate
parameter, yields a similar family of functions.

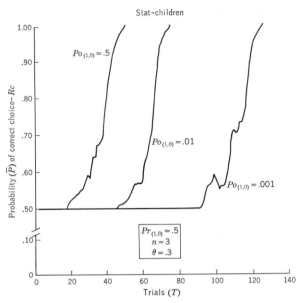

FIG. 8: Backward discrimination learning curves
for three groups of stat-children varying in initial
probability of attending to the relevant dimension.

poor discrimination learning of retardates is controlled by their
initial inattention to relevant stimulus dimensions.

The similarity in form of the functions of Figure 8 and those in
Figure 4 leads us again to the inference that initial probabilities of
observing different stimulus dimensions account for the variation in
discrimination learning of these stimulus dimensions. The same
argument is used to account for the data from the three transfer conditions: intradimensional shift, reversal, and extradimensional shift.
Each of these three transfer experiments is characterized by a different
pair of probabilities: (1) of correct attention at the beginning of
transfer $(Po_{(1,0)})$ and (2) instrumental approach to the positive
cue $(Pr_{(1,0)})$. These probabilities are evaluated in Figure 9, which
also shows the stat-child performances generated for each experimental
condition. The correspondence of stat-child predictions with the
retardate data of Figure 5 we assume is not accidental.

On at least one occasion, theoretical *predictions* have been made
in the temporal as well as logical sense. With certain combinations
of parameter values oddly shaped discrimination reversal curves were
predicted by the computer before we had examined the data appro-

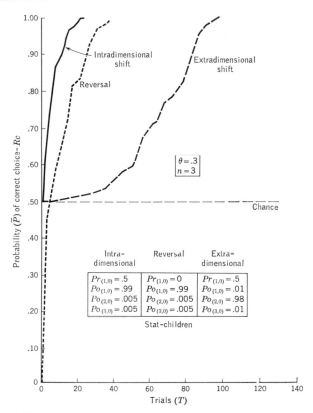

Fig. 9: Theoretical curves for intradimensional-shift, reversal, and extradimensional-shift problems. Performances of three groups of twenty stat-children are plotted as backward learning curves except for the first two points of each function, which come from forward learning curve calculations. The lateral positioning of the curves is that of the median subject in each group. Parameter values common to all three curves are indicated, as are the distinctive parameters for each condition.

priate for this particular combination of parameters. Figure 10 shows an approximation of stat-child performance during reversal in which a peculiar plateau occurs in the middle of the reversal. We were surprised at this prediction. We went looking for empirical support for it. The reversal midplateau has been found in both retardate data and the data of at least three other classes of subjects. Figure 11 is a sample of a reversal midplateau for retardates learning to reverse

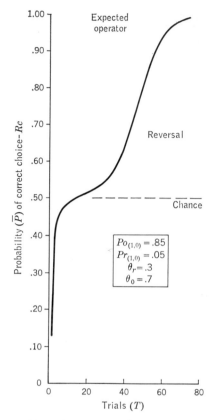

FIG. 10: Expected operator approximation of a theoretical reversal function with parameter values that accentuate the reversal mid-plateau.

a position discrimination. Further elaborations of this theoretical model continue to be consistent with empirical data (House and Zeaman, 1963; Zeaman and House, 1963).

I would like to conclude with this observation. We find an attention theory of retardate discrimination learning to be both exciting and amiable because it relates the poor performance of retardates on discriminative tasks to experimentally manipulable factors related to attention. Such a theory ought to be of use to behavioral engineers and educators. We think the theory is at least true for retardates, but probably not uniquely true for them.

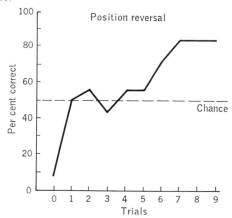

FIG. 11: Position reversal data for a group of twenty-four retardates.

REFERENCES

HARLOW, H. F. The formation of learning sets. *Psychol. Rev.*, 1949, **56**, 51–65.

HAYES, K. J. The backward curve: a method for the study of learning. *Psychol. Rev.*, 1953, **60**, 269–275.

HOUSE, B. J. The effect of distinctive responses on discrimination reversals in retardates. *Amer. J. ment. Defic.*, 1964, **69**, 79–85.

HOUSE, B. J., & ZEAMAN, D. Transfer of a discrimination from objects to patterns. *J. exper. Psychol.*, 1960, **59**, 298–302.

———. Miniature experiments in the discrimination learning of retardates. In L. P. Lipsitt & C. C. Spiker (Eds.), *Advances in child development and behavior*. New York: Academic Press, 1963.

HULL, C. L. The place of innate individual and species differences in a natural-science theory of behavior. *Psychol. Rev.*, 1945, **52**, 55–60.

JARVIK, M. E. Simple color discrimination in chimpanzees: effect of varying contiguity between cue and incentive. *J. comp. physiol. Psychol.*, 1956, **49**, 492–495.

KENDLER, H. H., & KENDLER, T. S. Vertical and horizontal processes in problem solving. *Psychol. Rev.*, 1962, **69**, 1–16.

RESTLE, F. A theory of discrimination learning. *Psychol. Rev.*, 1955, **62**, 11–20.

SPENCE, K. W. *Behavior theory and learning.* Englewood Cliffs, N.J.: Prentice-Hall, 1960.

WERNER, H. *Comparative psychology of mental development.* (Rev. ed.) Chicago: Follet, 1948.

WYCKOFF, L. B., JR. The role of observing responses in discrimination learning. Part I. *Psychol. Rev.*, 1952, **59**, 431–442.

ZEAMAN, D., & HOUSE, B. J. An attention theory of retardate discrimination. In N. R. Ellis (Ed.), *Handbook of mental deficiency*. New York: McGraw Hill, 1963.

ZEAMAN, D., HOUSE, B. J., & ORLANDO, R. Use of special training conditions in visual discrimination learning with imbeciles. *Amer. J. ment. Defic.*, 1958, **63**, 453–459.

7

DIAGNOSTIC, CULTURAL, AND REMEDIAL FACTORS IN MENTAL RETARDATION

Samuel A. Kirk

Mental retardation is not a new phenomenon; it has existed as long as man. The prevention, cure, care, management, and education of the mentally retarded have, however, remained as persistent problems which have defied solution.

The first modern major attempt at the education of the mentally retarded known to us was initiated with the classic work of Itard. I would like to recommend to the reader Itard's book, *The Wild Boy of Aveyron,* which has been out of print for many years, but has recently been reprinted in English (1962). It is a classic work in psychology, because the author relies on psychological techniques and principles in training Victor, the Wild Boy of Aveyron.

In the nineteenth and early twentieth centuries the influential educators of the mentally retarded were not professional teachers but came primarily from the field of medicine. Itard was an otologist and a physician. He is best known, however, not for his work in the field of otology and auditory training, where he made contributions, but for work benefiting the education of the mentally retarded. His contribution classifies him as an educator rather than a physician, if we define an educator as one who advances education. Edward Seguin followed Itard in the education of the mentally retarded. He was originally a teacher and then became a physician. His contribution

SAMUEL A. KIRK, Ph D., is director of the Institute for Research on Exceptional Children, University of Illinois.

was primarily in the development of the physiological method of teaching the retarded. Seguin, like Itard, was a physician who had done significant work in developing methods of educating the mentally retarded.

Another major contribution to the education of the mentally retarded was made by Maria Montessori (reprint, 1964). As a pediatrician, she accepted as patients retarded children who were referred to her. Having no appropriate medical treatment for them, Dr. Montessori resorted to environmental-educational methods of treatment. As a result of her work she became, not a great physician, but a great educator. As is well known, the Montessori method has had a lasting influence as a method of teaching not only the mentally retarded but also young normal children.

During the early part of the twentieth century another physician, Decroly, came into prominence as an educator in Belgium and France. Like Montessori, he developed materials and methods for teaching purposes. These were known as the Decroly materials. His student, a psychologist, Alice Descoeudres, elaborated on the Decroly procedures and published an important, but little known book, entitled *The Education of Mentally Defective Children* (1928).

The contributions of Itard, Seguin, Montessori, and Decroly to education serve to emphasize the interdisciplinary origins of the educational methods for mentally retarded children. Following the original contributions of the physicans, psychologists like Descoeudres entered the field and continued the work of developing educational programs for the mentally retarded.

One of the earliest psychologists to show an interest in this field was Alfred Binet. He is known in this country as an experimental psychologist who developed an intelligence test. Binet's primary interest in developing the test was for use in evaluating the performance of school children. He wrote a book, entitled *Modern Ideas About Children* (1909), in which part of one of his chapters dealt with "The Educability of Intelligence." In this chapter he said ". . . after the evil, the remedy, after exposing mental defects of all kinds, let us pass on to their treatment" (1909, p. 140). Thus, Alfred Binet sought to establish educational programs as a sequel to the development of his intelligence test. He organized special classes in France, which followed an instructional program not only for training the children in social adjustment or in reading, writing, and arithmetic, but also for the specific purpose of developing their intelligence. He believed that appropriate programs would develop memory, logic, verbal ability, attention, and other psychological functions. In this manuscript he described the teaching techniques that he believed would accelerate mental development. He was, as he stated, seeking an educational method which would be a "remedy." Interestingly, he called the educational method "mental orthopedics."

American psychologists eagerly adopted Alfred Binet's intelligence test. We are still using it as the major instrument for the assessment of intellectual ability. But psychologists in this country forgot that Binet's interest in the measurement of intelligence was primarily for identifying intellectual defects and modifying intelligence through training. Thus, it is obvious that Binet did not believe that the IQ was constant, that a child was destined to maintain a certain level of intelligence for the rest of his life.

In this country a special factor contributed to the neglect of Binet's work on the educability of intelligence. This was the research on the inheritance of feeble-mindedness. Goddard's studies on the Kallikak family (1914), for example, were interpreted as showing that mental deficiency was inherited, that 80 per cent of mental retardation was genetically determined and could not be significantly modified through training.

These conclusions had a very profound effect on the development of educational programs for the retarded in this country. Educators believed that if the mentally retarded could not use their heads, they would accept that fact and use their hands. Consequently, most educational programs were designed for what might be called compensatory education. Special classes and institutional programs included in their curricula training in basket weaving, rug making, and other manual activities. While these activities are valuable as new experiences, after the seventh or eighth rug the educational benefits decrease, and in a sense the activity becomes a "spinal reflex," rather than a learning experience. Those institutional administrators who boasted that some of their children had woven eight rugs actually did not have an educational program, but a production line of "busy work."

Because of Binet's influence and my desire to do more than just teach retarded children to read, or to focus only on social adjustment, I have been a bit persistent in thinking that there is a possibility of accelerating the rate of mental development by training abilities of retarded children. This view has been encouraged by such work as that of Skeels and Dye (1939), and by studies in animal psychology. The work of Lashley, for example, demonstrated that rats could make complex visual discriminations in the right situation. There is repeated evidence to show that if we know how to present the materials and how to manipulate the environment, training of the retarded child is possible. Hence, we may be able to do more than follow the fatalistic approach that is implicit in certain definitions of mental deficiency, to wit, that the condition exists at birth, that it is constitutional, and incurable. Such descriptions imply that there is not much we can do about it but to live with it. It has been gratifying to do something else with the retarded besides teaching them routine habits and skills. In this connection I should like to describe a few experiments.

AN EXPERIMENT IN PRESCHOOL EDUCATION

At the outset it was postulated that if education were started with very young children (excluding extreme clinical types), training and experience could very possibly accelerate the rate of mental development and prevent some cases of mental retardation. This, of course, was merely a hypothesis, as we had not yet tried systematic training at this level. To conduct these experiments we worked with groups of mentally retarded children below the age of six. In several experiments we offered preschool education to some and left others without training. Follow-up studies after three or four years indicated that preschool education had some effect on social and mental development.

The method of evaluating significant change in rates of development involved first classifying the children into certain categories or channels of development, as is done on the Wetzel grid (1946) for physical development. The categories of intellectual development used were: average, low average, borderline, high educable, low educable, and uneducable.

Figure 1 presents the categories employed. It had been previously assumed that once a child was in the low educable group, for example, he would remain in that channel throughout his life. We hypothesized, however, that environmental intervention could displace the rate of growth to the next higher channel, or to a lower one. The children in the experiment were evaluated by psychologists following intensive testing and were classified according to these channels. After a period of preschool training, the children were re-examined to determine whether there had been a significant change in the rate of development. Data from a few of these experiments, which were conducted with different groups of children, will be presented.

Table 1 presents the results of an experiment with twenty-six mentally retarded children (Kirk, 1962). Four of these were in foster homes and the balance in their own homes.

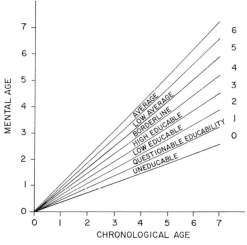

Fig. 1: Mental growth grid.

The four foster home children were placed in these homes by social agencies at the ages of three to five because of extreme neglect by parents who had abandoned them for one reason or another. In addition to foster home placement they were enrolled in the pre-school. It will be noted from Table 1 that all of these four children

TABLE 1: Effect of Preschool and Foster Home Experience on Rate of Intellectual Development

	Foster Home plus Preschool Education (No. = 4)		Experimental Preschool Children (No. = 12)		Twins and Sibling Controls (No. = 14)	
	No.	Ratio	No.	Ratio	No.	Ratio
Increased in rate of development	4	1.0	8	.67	2	.14
Held original rate of development	0	0.0	3	.25	7	.50
Decreased in rate of development	0	0.0	1	.08	5	.36

increased in rate of development. One child increased his rate of development three levels, from low educable to average, one child increased two levels, and the other two children increased one level each. This is a significant change in rate of mental and social development.

The group of twelve children, entitled Experimental Preschool Children, and a group of fourteen, entitled Twins and Sibling Controls, were living in their own homes. All twenty-six children came from extremely disadvantaged homes. Twelve children were admitted to the experimental preschool at an average age of four and one-half years, while their fourteen sibling and twin controls were left at home. After age six both the experimental and control children were admitted to regular or special schools and followed for two to three years. The results are summarized below.

Eight out of the twelve children enrolled in the preschool increased their rate of development. Three children remained at the same level and one child dropped in rate of development. It is interesting to note that the last child is one who came from a home in which the mother seemed unable to prepare him for his taxi transportation by nine o'clock each morning. As a result, he attended the preschool only half of the time.

The rate of development of the control group, consisting of fourteen twins and siblings,[1] was different. Out of the fourteen children in this group, two increased in rate of development without preschool experience, seven maintained their rate of development, and five dropped in rate of development to a lower channel.

Figure 2 gives a graphic comparison of the three groups. The graph presents the mean change in rate of development of each group in terms of the levels described in Figure 1. Thus, for example, the four children placed in foster homes and attending the preschool increased a total of seven levels, or a mean of 1.75 levels, as shown in Figure 2.

From these data we may draw the following conclusions.

1. Children from psychosocially deprived homes can accelerate their rate of mental and social growth if placed in foster homes and given preschool education.

2. Children who remain in their psychosocially deprived homes but are given preschool education tend to increase in rate of develop-

[1] An attempt was made to obtain twins for this experiment, but only two retarded pairs were found in the community. For that reason siblings a year or so older or younger were used as sibling controls.

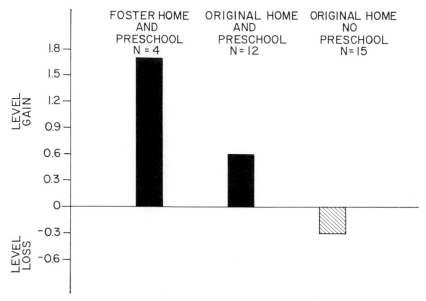

FIG. 2: Average change in levels of development as a function of pre-school and foster home experience.

ment, but not to the extent of those placed in foster homes and offered preschool education.

3. Children who remain in their psychosocially disadvantaged homes without preschool experience but who attend school after the age of six tend either to retain their rate of growth, or to drop in rate of growth.

Another similar experiment was conducted in two institutions for the mentally retarded (Kirk, 1958). Fifteen children between four and five years of age with IQ's between forty-five and sixty-five were selected from the wards of one institution and placed in a school organized especially for them. Twelve children with similar IQ's and chronological ages were identified in the second institution, but no provision for schooling was made. At age six, both groups attended their respective institution schools. The two groups were then compared on the rates of development through the ages of seven and one-half years.

Figure 3 presents the mental and social age growth curves on three tests: (a) the Stanford-Binet Scale, (b) the Kuhlmann Test of Mental Development, and (c) the Vineland Social Maturity Scale. The upper curve in Figure 3 (left) represents the Stanford-Binet

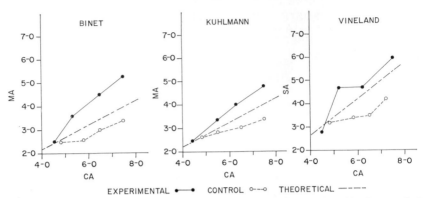

Fig. 3: MA and social age growth curves of institutionalized retarded children as a function of preschool experience.

mental age (MA) obtained at chronological ages (CA) 4–4 to 7–4 for the fifteen children offered preschool education. The dotted line in the middle is a theoretical line which represents the MA for the twenty-seven children comprising the experimental and control groups, assuming the IQ to be constant. These curves show that the fifteen children who were trained in a preschool experienced an accelerated rate of mental development as compared to the theoretical growth curve. On the other hand, the twelve children who did not receive preschool training, whose development is represented on the lower curve, dropped in rate of mental growth between the age of four and eight, when compared to the theoretical curve. On the Kuhlmann Test of Mental Development, the same differences were obtained—an acceleration of the fifteen children who received preschool training and a drop among the twelve children who did not receive preschool training. On the Vineland Social Maturity Scale similar results were obtained. Acceleration in social age (SA) was characteristic of the group that received training and a drop in rate of development occurred in the group that did not receive training.

The actual changes in IQ and SQ (social quotient) are presented graphically in Figure 4 for each of the tests. The children who received training improved significantly on each of the tests. In the control group the children who remained in the wards dropped in IQ and SQ on all tests.

Perhaps a more crucial measure than the IQ is the difference brought about in the life situation. The most practical result of the experiment was that of the fifteen children who attended preschool

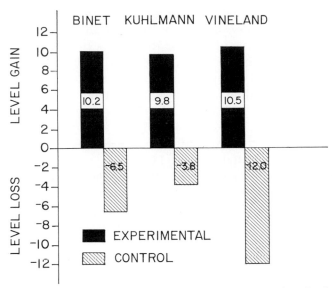

Fig. 4: IQ and SQ change scores of institutionalized
retarded children as a function of preschool experience.

seven were paroled from the institution by the age of six. The children
were paroled either to their own homes or to foster homes. Of the
seven children who were paroled, only one returned to the institution, while the remaining six remained out of the institution in
further follow-up studies. Two of them turned out to be normal; one
is a third-year high school student now, making "B" and "C" grades
at the age of seventeen. Of the twelve control children who remained
in the institution, not a single one was paroled.

This experiment, plus a number of other experiments in England
and in this country (McCandless, 1964), indicates that it is possible
we are often too easily discouraged with retarded children. If we
start at an early enough age we may be able to accelerate the development of these children a little more than we had previously thought
possible. It is very likely, too, that if we discover the variables related
to this acceleration in mental growth, we may do better than we
have done in this and other experiments. Frankly, we are struggling
to find an appropriate technique and are searching for the important
variables in the development of conceptualization in children at an
early age.

I do not wish to give the impression that preschool education can
produce miracles. But it does appear to be a form of environmental

intervention that stimulates children to develop mentally and socially at a slightly higher rate than some have in an unstimulating home environment. It may be unrealistic to expect a complete cure.

It may be instructive to take a closer look at the children comprising the experimental group in the study illustrated in Figures 3 and 4. Of the fifteen children in this group, seven did not have a definitive medical diagnosis of pathology. They were committed to an institution because they achieved a low IQ on an intelligence test with etiology labeled as "cultural-familial," since no more definitive medical diagnosis could be established. The other eight children had a diagnosis of brain damage or some other specific pathology. When the experimental results were analyzed according to these variables, it was found that the children who did not have a definitive medical diagnosis of brain pathology made more progress in development than did those who had central nervous system involvement. These observations led to a search for greater specificity in training techniques appropriate to the two broad diagnostic groups of retardates.

DIAGNOSIS AND REMEDIATION OF SPECIAL DISABILITIES

There has been considerable discussion in this country about the education of brain-injured children. From these discussions it has been possible to isolate a number of concrete questions: (a) are cultural-familial mental retardates more amenable to improvement through preschool education than brain-injured children; (b) why was preschool education not as effective as a training tool with the organically injured group; (c) what are the more appropriate methods of training this group of children? In searching for answers to these questions it seemed appropriate first to select a behavioral framework to serve as a model against which the capabilities and deficits of the retarded children could be evaluated. After careful investigation, we decided to look in the area of communication theory. This area seemed especially appropriate since mental retardation is primarily a language, speech, conceptual, and perceptual problem.

The model that was finally selected, because of its direct bearing on our work, was derived and adapted from the formulations of Charles Osgood (1957). A practical model of the communication process is presented in Figure 5. This figure ". . . presents the three dimensions of the model; namely, (a) channels of communication (auditory input, vocal output, and visual input, motor output); (b) levels of organization (automatic-sequential and representational); and (c)

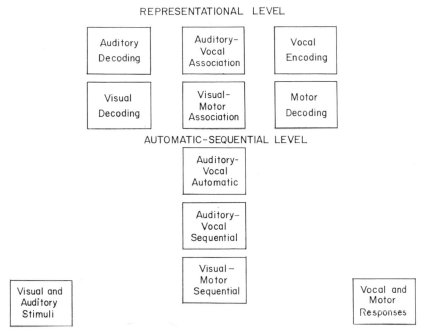

FIG. 5: A model of the communication process.

psycholinguistic processes (decoding, association, encoding)" (Kirk and McCarthy, 1961, p. 402).

Nine discrete tests were constructed to permit the evaluation of capacity for communication in each child. The tests were standardized on seven hundred children between the ages of two and nine and later published as the Illinois Test of Psycholinguistic Abilities (McCarthy and Kirk, 1961a). A brief description of the tests follows.

Auditory decoding measures ability to understand spoken language. This test requires "yes" or "no" answers or equivalent gestures to such questions as, "Do airplanes fly?"

Visual decoding measures ability to understand visual objects without the use of vocal response. The test requires the presentation first of a stimulus picture. After this has been removed, a set of four pictures is presented from which the child is to identify, by pointing, one picture like the stimulus picture.

Auditory-vocal association measures ability to associate verbal symbols. This is accomplished by the use of an analogies test, utilizing sentence completion: Father is big; baby is ——.

Visual-motor association measures ability to relate visual objects. This is accomplished by using a picture association test where the child is asked to select from a set of four pictures (by pointing) the one which goes with a stimulus picture, presented simultaneously.

Vocal encoding measures ability for vocal expression. In this test familiar objects, such as a ball or block, are presented to the child and he is asked, "Tell me all about this."

Motor encoding measures ability for expression in motor gestures. This is done by use of a gestural manipulation test. An object or picture is shown to the child and he is asked, "Show me what we should do with this."

Auditory-vocal automatic measures ability to respond in automatic or grammatical terms. This is assessed by a grammar test, with pictures as ancillary aids. The child completes the sentence: Here is a hat; here are two ———.

Auditory-vocal sequential measures auditory sequential memory. This is assessed by a digit repetition test.

Visual-motor sequential measures memory for sequential visual symbols. This test requires the child to duplicate the order of a sequence of pictures or geometrical designs which have been presented and then removed.

The theoretical background underlying this model of the communication process will not be elaborated here, since this has been discussed elsewhere (McCarthy and Kirk, 1961b). The administration of the Illinois Test of Psycholinguistic Abilities results in scores which can be profiled, so that intra-individual differences among abilities can be measured.

Such a procedure has diagnostic value for isolating the disabilities that require remediation. This procedure differs from that of an omnibus intelligence test which yields an MA or an IQ from which only a general classification is made. An IQ of seventy-five, for example, tells the examiner that the child is retarded in general intelligence but does not specify where the deficits lie so that amelioration may be effected. An analogy is found in reading examinations. The survey type reading achievement test informs the examiner of the level or the grade at which the child is reading. It yields no information about the specific difficulties the child may have in the reading process. To determine specific difficulties, diagnostic reading tests are administered when the survey test indicates difficulty. The Illinois Test of Psycholinguistic Abilities serves a similar purpose for the diagnosis of communication difficulties. Several illustrations of the usefulness of this test for the diagnosis of specific difficulties of retarded children are outlined below.

Figure 6 presents a profile of the test data on John. This boy had shown noticeable delay in talking and walking, and at age four had been excluded from a nursery school because of suspected retardation and social immaturity. His developmental history indicated that he crawled at eighteen months and walked at twenty-three months. He used two-word combinations at three years instead of the usual age of two years. The medical examination was negative. At age 4–4 he obtained an IQ of 79 on the Stanford-Binet.

Profile A represents the first examination of John at age 4–6. He obtained the highest scores in auditory decoding (1), visual decoding (2), auditory-vocal automatic (7), and auditory-vocal sequential (8). He scored low, or below norms of age two, on visual-motor association (4), motor-encoding (6), and the visual-motor sequential test (9). These deficits indicate the area in which John needs remediation.

Remediation was given this boy in the home, four times a week for four months. Training consisted of exercises in motor encoding, development of visual-motor association, and visual sequencing. At the end of four months he was re-examined. Profile B, which represents the first post-test, shows progress in many areas, and particularly in motor encoding. He was then tutored for an additional eight months (summer session intervening) and examined one year later. Profile C represents the results of the third examination. It should be noted that marked gains were made in the areas of disability: visual-motor association, motor and vocal encoding, and in visual sequencing. The other areas developed at or above the rate expected in normal growth.

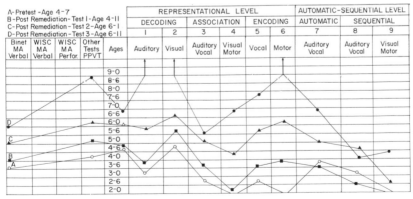

Fig. 6: Results of remediation.

Individual tutoring continued with this boy sporadically. In addition he was enrolled in a kindergarten with an experimental rhythmic and sensory-motor program. In this program he attended fifteen half-hour sessions over a period of five weeks.

The group training was geared to activities pertinent to body image, sensory-motor integrity, and psycholinguistic abilities. Activities were presented in nine of the twelve movement areas suggested by Barsch's Movegenic Theory (1963):

  a) visual dynamics (see and move),
  b) auditory dynamics (hear and move),
  c) dynamic balance (balance both sides of body),
  d) spatial awareness (awareness of one's body in space as a reference point),
  e) tactual dynamics (feel and move),
  f) body awareness,
  g) rhythm (movement to well-defined rhythmic patterns),
  h) unilateral and bilateral movement (move one side of body or two sides),
  i) flexibility (ability to change tempo, movement patterns, mood, etc.).

At the termination of this program, John had five one-hour psychodrama sessions. At the beginning of training he appeared withdrawn and unmotivated to move or play roles. He was encouraged to start by being required at first to perform rather simple activities for which he was reinforced, and then he progressed to more difficult movements. During the course of these sessions his attitude changed from withdrawal to active participation.

At this point John was again re-examined. Profile D in Figure 6 shows surprising acceleration in auditory decoding (1), visual decoding (2), and in his area of greatest deficit, motor encoding (6). His scores were now higher than expected for his chronological age. Auditory and visual sequencing, not touched in training during the latter period, now showed the greatest deficits. Parents and teachers also reported considerable improvement in this boy's abilities and in his successful participation in activities with other children. His last IQ at age 6–8 was 86 on the Binet, and his mental age on the Peabody Picture Vocabulary Test (PPVT) was 8–10. This performance was consistent with the level achieved on auditory and visual decoding.

The next case is Tommy, a ten-year-old boy in the fourth grade, who was referred for examination because of his difficulty in responding vocally and in writing. His classmates accepted him passively as a boy "who didn't talk." The teacher reported that in a discussion he raised his hand in class, but when called upon he either did not respond or responded in one-word sentences. One teacher reported that it seemed as though he wanted to say something but could not. He was able to give one- or two-word responses to discrete questions, or to repeat digits or sentences, but he was deficient in defining words or speaking spontaneously. Counseling was tried with the boy without success.

Results of psychometric examinations ranged from an IQ of 73 obtained on the Goodenough Draw-A-Man-Test to an IQ of 118 on the Wechsler Verbal Scale (excluding the vocabulary test on which he could not score) and 129 on the Peabody Picture Vocabulary Test. On reading, arithmetic, and language achievement tests he was scoring at the third-grade level.

Figure 7 presents the profile of Tommy on the Illinois Test of Psycholinguistic Abilities. It is apparent from the profile that this boy is extremely deficient in both vocal and motor encoding but near the top of the norms in most of the other tests.

Attempts were made to elicit vocal and motor responses from this boy in the classroom and also in a tutorial situation. The classroom teacher made an effort to assist him in vocal response by telling him a part of the sentence, asking him to repeat it and complete it. The tutor, with the aid of the Program Learning Laboratory and a com-

					REPRESENTATIONAL LEVEL						AUTOMATIC-SEQUENTIAL LEVEL		
					DECODING		ASSOCIATION		ENCODING		AUTOMATIC	SEQUENTIAL	
					1	2	3	4	5	6	7	8	9
Binet MA Verbal	WISC MA Verbal	WISC MA Perfor.	Other Tests PPVT	Ages	Auditory	Visual	Auditory Vocal	Visual Motor	Vocal	Motor	Auditory Vocal	Auditory Vocal	Visual Motor
				9-6									
	A			9-0									
				8-6									
				8-0									
				7-6									
				7-0									
				6-6									
				6-0									
				5-6									
				5-0									
				4-6									
				4-0									
				3-6									
				3-0									
				2-6									
				2-0									

FIG. 7: Results of remediation of an expressive disability.

puter, programmed assignments that could be fulfilled on a typewriter. Here again he was first given sentences which he could read orally, then sentences with a letter of a word missing, then sentences with a word or words missing, which he was required to supply. In addition, his vocal responses were recorded and played back to him for comment.

Profile A shows quite clearly the boy possesses normal intelligence but has a severe vocal and motor encoding disability, or a condition typical of expressive aphasia. Profile B shows the results of the post-test a year later, at the age of eleven. At this point there is evidence of much progress in encoding. The teacher reports that the boy has made marked improvement and that he is expressing himself in class to an extent not previously expected.

These and similar cases illustrate a clinical approach to the amelioration of learning disabilities in children, some of whom had been classified as mentally retarded. The attempt at specifying the nature of the deficit represents a decidedly different approach to the education of some of these children. This approach should not be construed as a substitute for training the children on the three R's and social adjustment. It does, however, introduce another dimension, namely training in aptitudes instead of achievements. Perhaps training in aptitudes should become another goal of education to be related to the educability of intelligence as measured by modern intelligence tests.

This approach consists primarily of behavioral analysis and behavioral treatment. For these purposes it is not necessary to determine whether or not a child has central nervous system involvement. It is important to determine the behavioral or functional abilities and disabilities, and to organize learning techniques that will ameliorate the behavioral deficits. Remediation in this context does not assume that biological structure or function is being changed or altered. It assumes that the child has potentialities in certain areas that have not been developed, due either to a biological defect or to avoidance of activity because of early failure. A child who has some difficulty in expressing himself verbally will tend to avoid verbal interaction and substitute a motor method of expression. Or, if he has some difficulty in visual interpretation, he may rely on auditory reception of information. As the child grows, the discrepancy between his ability in areas that are practiced and those that are avoided becomes greater. Special training on the deficits tends, therefore, to develop functions that should have developed earlier.

The management of the mentally retarded requires an educational program that will not only utilize the limited abilities of the mentally retarded but one that will also aim to ameliorate the areas of retarded function. Educational programs for mentally retarded children have traditionally concentrated on the development of skills, habits, attitudes, and personal and social adjustment. These are necessary but insufficient aims of education. Limited research indicates that much can be accomplished by utilizing the theories of the behavioral sciences in developing a scientific pedagogy. Evidence has been presented pointing to the value of early educational opportunities, and behavioral diagnosis and remediation in overcoming some of the handicaps associated with mental retardation.

REFERENCES

BARSCH, R. Project M.O.V.E. as a model for rehabilitation theory. Presented at Amer. Psychol. Ass. Convention, Philadelphia, 1963.

BINET, A. Les idées modernes sur les enfants. Paris: F. Flammarion, 1909.

DESCOEUDRES, ALICE. The education of mentally defective children. Transl. by E. F. Rom from 2d ed. Boston: Heath, 1928.

GODDARD, H. H. Feeblemindedness: its causes and consequences. New York: Macmillan, 1914.

ITARD, J. M. G. The wild boy of Aveyron. 1894. Transl. by G. & Muriel Humphrey, 1932. (Reprint) New York: Appleton-Century-Crofts, 1962.

KIRK, S. A. Early education of the mentally retarded. Urbana: Univer. of Illinois Press, 1958.

——. Effects of educational treatment. In R. L. Masland, R. F. Cooke, & L. C. Kolb (Eds.), Mental retardation. Res. publ. of Ass. Nerv. & Ment. Diseases, Vol. 39. Baltimore: Williams & Wilkins, 1962. Pp. 289–294.

KIRK, S. A., & MCCARTHY, J. J. The Illinois Test of Psycholinguistic Abilities —an approach to differential diagnosis. Amer. J. Ment. Def., 1961, 66, 399–412.

MCCANDLESS, B. R. Environment and intellectual functioning. In H. A. Stevens & R. Heber (Eds.), Mental retardation—a review of research. Chicago & London: Univer. of Chicago Press, 1964. Pp. 175–213.

MCCARTHY, J. J., & KIRK, S. A. The Illinois Test of Psycholinguistic Abilities, experimental edition. Urbana: Univer. of Illinois Press, 1961a.

——. Examiner's manual, Illinois Test of Psycholinguistic Abilities, experimental edition. Urbana: Univer. of Illinois Press, 1961b.

MONTESSORI, MARIA. The Montessori method. 1894. Transl. by Anne E. George, 1912. (Reprint) New York: Schoken Books, 1964.

OSGOOD, C. E. Contemporary approaches to cognition; a behavioristic analysis. Cambridge, Mass.: Harvard Univer. Press, 1957.

SKEELS, H. M., & DYE, H. B. A study of the effects of differential stimulation on mentally retarded children. Proc. Amer. Assoc. Ment. Def., 1939, 44, 114–136.

WETZEL, N. C. Mass, volume, surface and energy relationships in human growth and their application to the problem of growth failure in children. Cleveland Engineering, 1946, 39, 5.

INDEX

THE BIOSOCIAL BASIS OF MENTAL RETARDATION
edited by: Sonia F. Osler and Robert E. Cooke

designer:	Edward King
typefaces:	Baskerville, Bernhard Modern
compositor:	Modern Linotypers, Inc.
printer:	John D. Lucas Printing Co.
paper:	Warrentown Plate
binder:	Moore & Co.
cover material:	Columbia Riverside Linen